Mindful Self-Compassion for Teens in Schools

A 16-Session Social and Emotional Skills Curriculum for Middle and High Schoolers

Karen Bluth, PhD

MINDFUL SELF-COMPASSION FOR TEENS IN SCHOOLS
Copyright © 2024 by Karen Bluth, PhD

Published by
PESI Publishing, Inc.
3839 White Ave
Eau Claire, WI 54703

Cover design by Amy Rubenzer
Interior design and layout by Michelle Lagaroos
Editing by Jenessa Jackson, PhD

ISBN 9781683737667 (print)
ISBN 9781683737674 (ePUB)
ISBN 9781683737681 (ePDF)

PESI Publishing
pesipublishing.com

In memory of Aunt Rose—and for my
cousins Beth and Morissa, for Evan, and for
all other hardworking teachers who spend
their lives dedicated to the well-being of youth.
This book is dedicated to you.

Table of Contents

List of Sessions

 Introduction

> "The challenges today's generation of young people face are unprecedented and uniquely hard to navigate. And the effect these challenges have had on their mental health is devastating.
>
> **—Vivek Murthy**

Let's be honest.

Being a teacher is *hard*. And being a teacher of teens is particularly hard—maybe one of the hardest jobs ever. I know because I was a teacher for almost 20 years, the last 10 or so with fifth graders in an overcrowded and underfunded inner-city elementary school.

It wasn't easy, but I loved it. Like so many of you, mostly what I loved was the relationships with my students. Those kids were endlessly interesting and so much fun. I was charmed by their innocence and sweet awkwardness as they adapted to the changes in both their bodies and their relationships to the world. By the thoughts they poured out into their writing. By the way they delved into new concepts they encountered in their classes or in books they were reading. On the brink of adolescence, they felt their fears, joys, insecurities, and beliefs so deeply. When they sensed they were being mistreated, watch out—it was like a volcanic uproar. When they felt snubbed by a friend, the depth of pain they felt was heart-wrenching to witness.

I don't think I ever had a student in middle school who truly felt comfortable in their own skin, although I sincerely doubt they recognized that unease in each other. Some put on a seemingly impenetrable tough exterior, while others stood on the edge of the crowd and were more timid, yet I think they were all painfully insecure, questioning so many aspects of themselves—most notably their self-worth.

From a developmental perspective, this makes sense. The early teen years are defined by a sudden hyperawareness of the self, which makes teens overly self-conscious. A teen can walk in a room and be convinced that everyone in the room is watching them. There's actually a term for this, which the psychologist David Elkind (1967) came up with—"the imaginary audience." The process going on in a teen's head is something like this: *Everyone is watching me. Everyone can see my every flaw. They are staring at my bad skin, I just know it. They can see that my eyes are too far apart and that I'm having such a bad hair day. I wish my mom would let me dye my hair. I should have worn those other jeans, these aren't as cool. No wonder no one likes me. I'm so uncool. No wonder I feel so alone.*

Self-criticism runs rampant in these middle school years, as does the drive for perfectionism. But we can't all have perfect skin, keep up with the trendiest hair styles, get perfect grades, be great musicians, be insanely creative artists, and excel at sports. Setting the bar that high is unrealistic and sets us up for failure and disappointment, which is why perfectionism is often linked with greater depression in teens. High school

viii • Mindful Self-Compassion for Teens in Schools

is no better and, in fact, is often worse. Cliques wreak havoc during this time, and being excluded can be so traumatic that, years later, adults often recall painful words and actions that were launched at them in their high school years.

Being a teen has never been easy, mind you, but in today's world, it's harder than ever. In years past, teens certainly had ways of excluding others—whether it was through hallway whispers, lunchroom gossip, or bullying on the school bus—but social media has taken meanness to an entirely new level. As one school principal expressed to me, "It doesn't stop. When I was a kid, I could be picked on at school, but I knew once I got home and closed my front door, I was safe. No one could hurt me. Now it's totally different. There's no safe place for these kids. They're constantly subjected to any attack, at any time, from social media."

And let's face it, hostility, divisiveness, dishonesty are at an all-time high among political leaders, community members, and others in the public arena. Fully grown adults are hurling hateful insults at each other like it's nobody's business, so it comes as no surprise that name-calling, something we would never allow on elementary school playgrounds, has become the norm. This is not to mention that mass shootings, including school gun violence, have skyrocketed in recent years, so much so that we hardly bat an eye when we hear that another dozen or so have been killed in yet another tragedy.

This is not a healthy environment to live in. Not for adults, not for teachers, and certainly not for teens.

What can we do to help teens navigate this developmentally challenging period of life? How can we offer them a hand as they traverse the rocky terrain of the teen years, which has become even rockier in the current political and social climate?

Luckily, there is something that can help, and you have a guide to it in your hands. It's called self-compassion, which involves treating yourself with kindness and support when you're having a hard time, just the way you would treat a good friend. We know from research studies that teens and adults who practice self-compassion are less stressed, anxious, and depressed, and they're often more resilient and happier with their lives, even in the face of challenges (Marsh et al., 2018; Pullmer et al., 2019). We also know that people can "grow" self-compassion through specific practices and skills that help them approach their struggles with the same kindness, respect, and support that they give to others.

That's what this book is all about—teaching teens how to be kinder and more supportive to themselves— how to stop being mean to themselves—so they can better cope with whatever comes their way.

What Is in This Book

In this book, I've provided you with everything you need to know to teach self-compassion to students in a classroom or small group setting. Whether you're a teacher, counselor, instructional aide, administrator, or any other type of educator working with teens, this book offers ready-to-use and reproducible self-compassion lessons that were created and formatted to be taught in middle or high school classrooms.

In chapter 1, I provide a more detailed definition of self-compassion and describe the research illustrating the benefits of self-compassion on mental health. In chapter 2, I explain how to approach teaching self-compassion in classroom settings, with special consideration for adolescent development, so that you can get the best possible results.

Chapter 3 describes how to conduct inquiry, which is the process by which students reflect on their experience of doing a guided self-compassion practice. Chapter 4 is devoted to the actual self-compassion curriculum—a series of 16 lessons, 45–50 minutes each, that are designed to be taught sequentially over the course of a semester. This curriculum has been adapted from Kristin Neff and Christopher Germer's Mindful Self-Compassion program for adults and a program I co-created, called Mindful Self-Compassion for Teens.

Chapter 5 provides 10-to-15-minute "mini lessons" that educators can introduce to students at any time during the school year. I created these mini lessons after hearing from several school counselors that they only had limited time to introduce a concept or practice when visiting the classroom. Some of these mini lessons were created as standalone drop-in sessions, while others are lessons within the 16-session curriculum that can be taught as mini lessons (either on their own or sequentially over several weeks).

Chapter 6 wraps up the book by giving recommendations on where teachers can go from here, including how to respond to questions that school administrators or parents might have about self-compassion.

Finally, the appendices provide additional information that will help you teach this program. Appendix 1 has a list of supplementary resources, appendix 2 contains all the worksheets for the 16-session curriculum, and appendix 3 provides four scales that allow you to assess students' progress before and after participating in the program.

This self-compassion curriculum aligns with the Collaborative for Academic, Social, and Emotional Learning (CASEL) framework that supports the integration of social and emotional skills into the classroom (Devaney et al., 2006). Within the Multi-Tiered System of Supports (MTSS) framework, *Mindful Self-Compassion for Teens in Schools* works well as a universal Tier 1 program taught in the classroom and as a preventative Tier 2 intervention provided to small groups by school counselors. It is targeted to 11-to-18-year-olds, although we never teach that age span together in one group but, rather, teach groups with a smaller age range, such as 11-to-14-year-olds or 15-to-18-year-olds. We have found that the curriculum works well across all these ages, with only minor changes in manner of delivery.

And so the opportunity has fallen in your lap—*you* can be the person who turns around teens' lives by teaching them these critical coping skills that they can take with them and have in their back pocket for the rest of their lives.

Want to learn how? Turn the page . . .

PART 1

Welcome to the Journey of Teaching Self-Compassion

CHAPTER 1

What Is Self-Compassion?

> 66 Whoever our students may be, whatever the subject we teach, ultimately we teach who we are.
>
> **—Parker J. Palmer**

Simply put, self-compassion is a kind and supportive way of treating yourself. It is a resource that we all have to some degree—we would not have survived to this point in our lives if we didn't have at least some self-compassion! But it can also be a momentary state of being—for example, when you recognize that you're struggling and take a moment to comfort or support yourself. Perhaps you put on your favorite music, go for a walk, or simply console yourself with a few kind words.

To understand what self-compassion is, it's best to take a look at what compassion is, which is a concept that people are often much more familiar with. Compassion involves recognizing the suffering of others and feeling compelled to alleviate that suffering. When you pass an unhoused person on the street, hear about victims of war on the news, or see commercials of children who are enduring the seemingly impossible process of cancer treatment, and you feel moved to do something—that's compassion. As an educator, you feel compassion every day for your students. You wouldn't still be at your job if you didn't. And you certainly wouldn't be reading this book if you didn't care and didn't have the desire to make life easier for your students.

Self-compassion isn't very different from compassion. It's simply taking that compassion you feel for others and making a U-turn by extending that compassion toward yourself. This is a radical idea in our culture, where we are raised to be compassionate toward others but not necessarily ourselves. It's what we all hear growing up—be kind to others. Treat others with respect. Give to those less fortunate. Be a loyal friend. Take care of others in need. Treat others the way you would want to be treated.

Yet oddly enough, we don't treat ourselves with the same kindness and respect that we so readily give to others. In fact, we do the *opposite*. When we're struggling and having a bad day, we tend to be shockingly self-critical and think of a million ways we could have done or said things differently. We say horribly harsh things

3

to ourselves that we would never dare say to anyone else. To top it off, many of us go on like this for days, ruminating endlessly about how we are such a terrible person for acting the way that we did.

But it doesn't have to be this way. We can learn to treat ourselves differently. We can learn to treat ourselves with the same respect, kindness, and support with which we treat others. And we can teach our students to do the same.

Three Components of Self-Compassion

According to self-compassion pioneer and researcher Dr. Kristin Neff (2003), the formal definition of self-compassion comprises three different components—mindfulness, common humanity, and self-kindness. In the context of self-compassion, **mindfulness** means having a balanced perspective when things don't go well. You don't exaggerate the importance of the situation that went awry, yet you also don't brush it aside or shove it under the rug either. In this context, mindfulness means simply noticing and acknowledging what you're feeling right now. For example, in the face of difficulty, you might say to yourself, "Wow, I'm feeling super angry" or "I'm feeling frustrated. I've explained this concept to students several times, and they're just not getting it. I'm not sure what I should do next!"

How does mindfulness "work"? Simply put, when left to its own devices, the mind will naturally wander. That wouldn't be such a problem, except that minds tend to wander to places that cause us worry. At times, our minds wander to the past, and we ruminate obsessively about something we said or did that we regret. Other times, our minds wander to the future, and we worry about everything that could possibly go wrong in our lives. For students, this could be an upcoming exam, a friend who has ghosted them, or a conflict with a parent.

Why do we do this? Our minds are trying to protect us. When we're rehashing the past, the mind is trying to protect us from making the same mistake again, and when it's dwelling on the future, it's planning how we're going to handle the situation if it goes awry. But let's face it, there's always something to worry about if we allow ourselves to go that route. And generally, there are a whole lot of things to choose from.

When you practice mindfulness, you train your mind to focus its attention on what's happening in the present moment instead of getting caught up in the past or future. You'll find that the curriculum in this book helps students practice mindfulness by noticing their physical sensations—because the senses provide an anchor to the present moment.

Common humanity is the understanding that you are not alone in feeling difficult feelings. In fact, emotions like anger, frustration, sadness, loneliness, hurt, and grief are part of the experience of being human—we all feel these feelings at times. This may seem obvious, and in many ways it is. But when we're the ones in the throes of a difficult emotion—when we're consumed by anger or at our wit's end—we often feel like we're the only ones going through these emotions. Perhaps this has been the case for you. Perhaps there have been times at school when you've looked down the hall, and it seems like everyone else is having an easier time, and you're the only one who is struggling. In the moment, you forget that perhaps even yesterday or last week, that teacher down the hall was having a hard day and vented to you in the teachers' lounge.

Why do we tend to expect our lives to be smooth sailing all the time? In part, it's because we receive messages from the media and society that we're supposed to be happy all the time, and if we're not—watch out—it means that we're doing something gravely wrong in our lives or that we're permanently flawed. Of course, this sets us up to have unrealistic expectations. We think that if we're not happy all the time, if our students aren't excelling, if our own children aren't insanely joyous every moment, if our partners don't greet us with a big smile and a bouquet of flowers every evening when they come home, that we're somehow a failure. We forget that life is simply not like that. We forget that life is replete with ups and downs—with moments that are filled with gratitude and joy *and* moments that are filled with struggle and sometimes enormous pain. We forget that all these moments are integral parts of being alive.

Finally, the third component of self-compassion is **self-kindness,** or the act of treating yourself with support and tenderness when you are having a hard time. One of the most accessible ways to practice self-kindness is to ask yourself what you might say to a friend if they were facing a similar difficulty, and then say those words to yourself. For example, a teen who is struggling because they did poorly on an exam can consider what they might tell a friend in the same situation, like "It's okay, you'll do better next time" or "This test isn't everything. It's just one grade. You'll get through this!"

With self-kindness, you don't let yourself off the hook for making a mistake, mind you. You simply correct it without falling into that black hole of harsh self-criticism and telling yourself what an idiot you are for making the mistake. This step can be pretty difficult for most people who are new to the practice of self-compassion, simply because they're not used to it. It's like trying out any new skill for the first time. It feels awkward and uncomfortable at first. It may even feel strange or inauthentic. But with time and practice, self-kindness becomes less awkward and more natural. And after a while, it feels really good! After all, who wouldn't want to receive support and kindness instead of harsh self-criticism?

The self-compassion curriculum offered in this book teaches teens specific ways to take that step to be kind to themselves, even though it will feel uncomfortable at first. Once they learn to be present and aware of that discomfort, they often realize (much to their surprise!) that the discomfort isn't overwhelming. They realize that they can, in fact, feel the discomfort without it taking over their entire being.

Self-Compassion Works

The really great news about self-compassion is that it works. Over a decade of research has shown that self-compassion protects teens against the onslaught of the challenges they must face every day. Not only are teens with greater self-compassion less likely to get depressed as they get older or when they're stressed (Bluth et al., 2017; Lathren et al., 2019), but they're also less likely to self-injure (Xavier et al., 2016), less likely to develop poor self-esteem (Marshall et al., 2015), less likely to have negative mood from chronic academic stress (Y. Zhang et al., 2016), less likely to get depressed when bullied (H. Zhang et al., 2019), and less likely to be negatively affected by social media (Keutler & McHugh, 2022; Phillips & Wisniewski, 2021).

You get the idea. What's more is that these studies were conducted all over the world. From Australia to China, Spain to Israel, and Turkey to the United States, research has found that self-compassion seems to serve as a buffer for the many difficulties that teens face in today's world.

And yet there's still more good news—self-compassion can be cultivated and intentionally "grown." What do I mean by that? If you are one of the millions of people who didn't happen to come into this world with a whole lot of self-compassion, you can learn how to develop more of it. Moreover, when you practice self-compassion over time, you can strengthen this habit of treating yourself kindly until it eventually becomes your default mode when you're struggling. How do I know? For one, I'm a prime example. Through my own mindful self-compassion practice, my default has become being gentle with myself in times of difficulty. When I've had a hard day or find myself feeling "less than," I know I need to slow down, take care of myself, and do something nice for myself. For me, that could mean crawling into bed with a good book and a cup of Earl Grey tea. And trust me, this wasn't always my default!

But besides my own personal experience, research from our team at the University of North Carolina at Chapel Hill has shown that you can cultivate self-compassion. After teens participate in our self-compassion program, they are more resilient, better able to embrace new experiences, and more willing to take positive risks (Bluth & Eisenlohr-Moul, 2017; Bluth, Gaylord, et al., 2016; Bluth et al., 2023). Over and over, I've heard teens talk about how the program has made a huge difference in their lives and how it has allowed them to see themselves and the world differently. The realization that they can be kind and supportive to themselves and *still* be successful is shocking to them—and empowering.

I've had the privilege of introducing self-compassion to many students and educators over the last decade, and they have taught me how life-giving this practice is. A teen who was hospitalized for an eating disorder described the self-compassion program as "eye-opening." A school counselor who suffered from severe depression told me that she wouldn't be alive today had it not been for learning about the practice of self-compassion. But perhaps my favorite comment came from a 15-year-old boy who declared, "You know, I don't care if people don't like me—because I like me!"

We know unequivocally that self-compassion is good for us. It's like having a supportive friend with us—inside us—at all times. In fact, what teens learn in the very first session of the self-compassion curriculum is just that—that they have a kind, supportive, and loving voice within them. Perhaps it's been buried under layers of self-critical voices, but it's there—quiet, still, and waiting to be brought forth and heard.

With this book in your hands, you are now in the position to help them do just that.

CHAPTER 2

How to Approach Teaching Self-Compassion in the Classroom

> 66 One of the best guides to how to be self-loving is to give ourselves the love we are often dreaming about receiving from others.
>
> **—bell hooks**

Teaching self-compassion is different from teaching any other curriculum. Unlike math or writing, it isn't content-driven but experiential. Put succinctly, to practice self-compassion, you need to be able to recognize your own emotional state in the moment, particularly when you're experiencing a negative emotion like frustration, anger, hurt, or sadness, and give yourself the support and care that you need. That means it can only be learned by reflecting on your experience with the practice.

So how do you teach this to students?

First and foremost, you have to be able to practice self-compassion yourself. You have to know the ropes of being able to identify your own emotional state, particularly when you're experiencing a negative mood like frustration, anger, hurt, or sadness, and then take the necessary steps to give yourself the support and care you need. In other words, you have to embody self-compassion. There are no shortcuts here. It's tempting to say, "Oh well, I don't have time for that. My students need it more than I do." That may be true, but you simply can't teach it unless you do it yourself. I promise.

Think about teaching swimming, for example. Sure, you could give students diagrams showing the different types of strokes, tell them when to kick their feet, or tell them when to take a breath—all without getting in the water yourself. But truly, you can't teach someone how to swim unless you've been in the pool yourself and have felt the movement of the water against your arms as you do the breaststroke or have felt the pressure in your lungs as you hold your breath underwater. You have no idea how difficult it is to stay buoyant unless you've been in the water and experimented with different ways of staying afloat.

Self-compassion is similar. To teach it, you have to do it yourself. Only then will you become familiar with the nuances of the practice, particularly what it *feels* like. And unless you're in the self-compassion "pool" yourself, you won't be able to respond to some of the questions students may ask. Only through your experience will you be able to teach from a place of integrity. Teaching through anything less will not be authentic or effective, and chances are that students will pick up on the fact that you haven't been in the swimming pool.

And, trust me, self-compassion will make your life a whole lot easier, so although it might feel like one more task that you need to cross off your to-do list, I encourage you to see it as a way of nurturing yourself, as something that I'm guessing you don't do very often. Maybe then it will sound more than a bit attractive to you.

So what are some easy ways to learn self-compassion? To start, you can read the book *Self-Compassion for Educators* by Lisa Baylis. It's a great resource that is filled with all sorts of accessible practices to get you started on your self-compassion journey. journey. Lisa Baylis and I also worked together with Kristin Neff to create a "Self-Compassion for Educators" course that is taught through the Center for Mindful Self-Compassion (www.centerformsc.org). There are also lots of online workshops, courses, and drop-in meditation sessions led by certified self-compassion teachers through the Center for Mindful Self-Compassion. These and other resources are listed in appendix 1.

One more word about developing your self-compassion practice—it is a lifelong process. Learning how to be kind and supportive to yourself, especially in the midst of difficult situations, is ongoing. Of course, that doesn't mean you have to wait twenty years to start teaching self-compassion to students but, rather, that you understand that there will always be deeper layers of knowing yourself that you can access over time.

Think of it as peeling back the layers of an onion. The process of being present and attentive to yourself and your needs unfolds gradually with time. With continued practice, you are able to notice more quickly when you're struggling and attend to your emotions so you don't become reactive with others—or with yourself. You'll find that you don't lose your temper so easily, you catch yourself more quickly when you start berating yourself for some mistake you've made, you have more patience with others, you have greater appreciation and gratitude for what you have in life, you more easily forgive others—the list goes on. Simply put, you find that you lead your life with a bit more ease. As the former news anchor Dan Harris says in his book of the same name, you're "10 percent happier."

So let's say that you've established your own self-compassion practice. Now how do you start teaching self-compassion?

How to Approach Teaching Self-Compassion

Since the approach to teaching self-compassion must be different from the approach to teaching a content-driven class, you must *invite* teens to participate, not require them to do so. Let's face it, you can't "require" anyone to do a guided visualization or an exercise that requires reflection anyway. Students can sit with their closed eyes and *look* like they're participating, but pretending to participate and actually participating are two very different things. In addition, teens want to be able to make some decisions for themselves, so empowering them to do so through an invitational style gives them some sense of control.

This doesn't mean you can't have a direct approach with students. You can, and many students will appreciate direct instructions. But it does mean that when there is resistance, you don't force the issue. Instructions for working through resistance can look something like this:

> *We are going to do a guided practice now. If you are comfortable closing your eyes, feel free to do that, but you certainly don't have to close your eyes if you don't want to. You can always just keep your eyes partly closed and with a downward gaze so you're not distracted by things around you.*
>
> *Check in with your shoulders. Are they relaxed and away from your ears? How about your jaw? Is it relaxed?*
>
> [Now imagine that you look around the room and see a student giggling and distracting the student next to them. You look at her directly and, in a kind but clear voice, say the following.]
>
> *Layla, if you don't want to do this practice, that's okay. You can just sit there quietly. But you are not free to prevent someone else from doing it.*

I have found that when students are given the choice on whether or not to participate, they will eventually join in. Most of the time, they simply want the ability to make the choice themselves, and when they see their peers engaged and getting something out of the practice, they join in. What's more, by honoring their capacity to choose, students become more aware of what they need and give it to themselves in turn, which is self-compassion in action!

It is important to note that using an invitational approach extends to *home practice* as well. When teaching the curriculum, we—self-compassion teachers—make a point not to refer to home practice as "homework" because we do not want students to see it as a school assignment—as one more thing they feel like they have to do. Rather, we want them to view it as something they choose to do for themselves because it is nurturing, it is healthy, and it makes them feel good. In order for that to happen, they have to be allowed to make that choice for themselves.

At this point, I know what you may be thinking: *What if they never choose to do home practice?*

It's okay. Really. For starters, we know from studies that "informal" or in-the-moment practice—that which is done during the flow of the day when difficult moments come up—is effective in reducing stress and improving mental health (Fredrickson et al., 2019; Kakoschke et al., 2021; Manigault et al., 2021; Shankland et al., 2021). Anecdotally, we also know that even when students don't do what we call "formal" practice—setting aside 10 or 20 minutes a day to practice—they still benefit from the time they spend in class talking about self-compassion and doing the practices.

In general, we have found that most young people don't do a lot of formal practice, but they do engage in informal practice. As one student confessed to me on the last day of a six-week course, "You know, I really haven't practiced much at home—or at all, really—but my perspective on how I see the world has changed." Changes can happen simply from being present in a self-compassion class and hearing about a different way of being with yourself.

Shifting to this hands-off approach may be somewhat challenging for educators who are used to assigning homework and applying demerits when assignments aren't completed. It's hard to let go of the enforcer role when you've been doing that for years and when it works with traditional academic content. But trust me, the invitational approach works. And if you keep in mind that there really isn't a choice—you can't make someone do a contemplative practice anyway—it becomes easier to step away from the controls.

How to Transition to a Self-Compassion Class

You want your students to understand that learning how to be compassionate toward themselves is different from any other content they learn in school. To get this message across right from the start, you'll need to make slight, but perceptible, changes to the classroom setting. Of course, you want these changes to be practical and doable, so I'm not going to tell you to move your class to the airy and incense-infused yoga studio down the road or even to rearrange your classroom. However, even small changes can make a difference. Here are some examples of things you can do:

1. Dim the lights or turn off the overhead lights completely, and use a floor lamp for softer light.

2. Minimize any distractions. You probably want to close the door to the hallway. You may want to make the main office aware of what you're doing so they can minimize any nonemergency alerts over the public address system.

3. Play soft music to transition to the "self-compassion space." Music can be a very effective vehicle for conveying the message that what's happening next is going to be different, particularly if the music creates a mood of relaxation, reflection, and rest. You may want to use a piece of music that you only play at the start of self-compassion class so that when students hear it, they know that it's time for self-compassion. (Music can also be used as a practice in itself, which I will discuss in part 2 of this book.)

4. If possible, move to a corner of the room (or a quiet corner of the school library or another space) that is carpeted and where pillows might be available. If this isn't possible, students can use pillows on their chairs or sit on carpet squares in a corner of the room. Be aware that moving to a different physical space outside of the classroom may be really helpful for students who have had academic challenges (Bluth, Campo, et al., 2016). As one student told me in the final class of their program, "It didn't work in the classroom. That's where we failed and stuff."

Overall, you want the atmosphere to convey a sense of emotional safety—of comfort, acceptance, warmth, and openness—where students are more open to being vulnerable. In my experience, I've become increasingly aware of how the physical space can make a striking difference. Years ago, I taught a self-compassion class to a group of adults in the community room of a swim club. The chairs were plastic and hard, the floor was tiled, and there was an icemaker that kept going on and off throughout class. Everything about the space felt stark and cold. It was not conducive to learning self-compassion, and interestingly (and quite unusually), we had several people drop out of the class partway through. I think they experienced the same vague sense of coldness that my co-teacher and I did.

5. Use mindful art activities to transition from traditional school content to the self-compassion space. The art activities can be brief—just 5 or 10 minutes long—and yet they quickly allow students to relax and move into a more reflective space. As students become more familiar with mindfulness, you can give instructions during these art activities that reinforce the practice of mindfulness, such as "Notice the feeling of the pencil in your hand" and "Notice the sound the pen makes as it comes in contact with the paper." Mindful art activities are included throughout the 16-session curriculum.

6. Mindful movement is another great way to transition from an academic class to a self-compassion class. Most of the learning in school happens from the neck up, but self-compassion brings an awareness to what is happening in our bodies when we experience emotions. Mindful movement allows students to make this transition from their heads to their bodies. As teens can be self-conscious about their bodies, keep instructions simple and straightforward. For example, you can first have students stand up, and then guide them to simply notice how their body feels, particularly after sitting in a chair for a time. They can notice which parts of their bodies feel stiff or cramped, and you can suggest that they respond by stretching these parts of their bodies. This can also be done while students are sitting in their chairs—it's about whatever works best for you and your students. Specific examples of mindful movement practices are provided in chapter 5 of this book as part of the drop-in lessons.

Working with an Assistant

It's always advantageous to have an extra pair of eyes and ears when teaching a classroom full of middle or high schoolers. It's even more important when teaching self-compassion. Although it is not the assistant's responsibility to make sure that students are engaging in the practice—remember, students are *invited* to participate—they should ensure that students aren't preventing others from participating. The assistant should also monitor students for signs of distress, as some self-compassion practices can be emotionally activating. Of course, assistants can attend to other tasks as well, such as distributing art supplies and addressing students' personal needs.

Ideally, the assistant should have at least some experience with mindfulness or self-compassion, as well as experience working with the age group that you're teaching. However, we don't live in an ideal world, so having a warm body available to simply monitor students while you're teaching can be enormously helpful. If you end up going with the "warm body" option, make sure that the assistant is well aware of the invitational approach to learning self-compassion so they can let go of the enforcer role.

Different Session Components and How to Approach Teaching Them

There are three different components to the self-compassion curriculum—topics, experiential exercises, and guided practices. **Topics** are conceptual introductions that provide an overview of what's being presented in that session. For example, the concept of how our minds have a tendency to wander is discussed in session 4. Teaching topics is pretty straightforward and probably the part of the program that you'll be most familiar with since it's the most similar to how you teach in school. The important thing to remember when teaching topics is to keep it brief, concise, and interactive. I'm sure you're well aware that students don't want to hear you drone on! If using humor and sharing stories come naturally to you, go for it. It brings a lightness to the sessions and makes it more fun.

Experiential exercises allow students to go through a process in which they access a felt sense of an emotion and also a felt sense of self-compassion. For example, in the *Motivating Ourselves with Compassion* exercise, students are able to experience and feel in their bodies what it's like to hear their harsh inner critical voice versus their inner compassionate voice. This exercise culminates in students generating a letter to themselves from the perspective of their compassionate voice. Through this process, they realize that not only is it possible to motivate themselves with self-compassion rather than self-criticism but that self-compassion feels a whole lot better too.

Before guiding students through an experiential exercise, it's important to familiarize yourself with the intention of the exercise, which is provided at the beginning of each instruction sheet. Each exercise is also carefully scripted to be trauma sensitive and safe, meaning they are designed to be taught in the classroom and not given for home practice. When leading an exercise, you (or your assistant) should monitor students for emotional arousal and adjust your tone and tempo accordingly to make sure it's within the students' "window of tolerance," or their ability to learn safely without becoming overwhelmed.

A slower tempo and a warmer tone will allow students to go more deeply into the experience, whereas a quicker tempo and more matter-of-fact tone will bring them somewhat out of the experience, which you will want to do if you notice them becoming activated. Know that becoming activated—getting a bit teary, for example—is not necessarily a bad thing. It means that students are accessing deeper parts of themselves and their experience. However, it may be more than you want to take on in a classroom when many other students are present. In a small group in a counseling setting, however, it may be perfectly suitable.

You can think of the "window of tolerance" as a series of concentric circles, with safety in the center ring, challenge in the next ring, and overwhelm in the outermost ring. **Safety** is the place where things feel familiar and where you feel calm and regulated. If you push yourself a bit and embrace new experiences, you move into the **challenge** zone. This is where most learning takes place. It's where you feel like you are stretching your mind, and maybe even your heart, to take in new information. **Overwhelm** is where things have gotten to be too much. You've been pushed too far out of your comfort zone and feel like you need a break. You may feel tired, burned out, frazzled, irritable, and maybe even like your head might explode.

However, you can protect yourself from moving into the overwhelm zone, and you can teach your students to do the same. When you learn to become aware of how you are feeling and the cues that your body is giving you, you can pace yourself and take care of yourself before you move into the territory of overwhelm. This may mean taking a break, getting some rest, or simply tuning out. That's self-compassion at work!

Remind students that it is really okay for them to stop the exercise at any point if it feels like it is too much for them. *This is being self-compassionate!* Knowing what you need and how to take care of yourself is the fundamental part of what you're teaching, so if a student starts feeling overwhelmed, it is perfectly fine for them to stop the practice and to give themselves what they need, whether it's feeling their feet on the floor, staring at the ceiling, or thinking about what they're having for lunch.

Finally, there are a few things to know when leading the **guided practices**. First, it's best to not refer to them as meditations. The word *meditation* is a loaded term that can mean many different things depending on someone's religious or spiritual background. Unless you are absolutely crystal clear about how the word will go over with your students, I'd stay away from it entirely. The word *practice* is perfectly fine.

When leading a guided practice, you'll want to "feel" the practice as you're doing it, while also keeping your eyes open so you can still monitor students. In other words, a part of you is *doing* the practice as you are leading it. This will help you know the pace to deliver it, as well as how long to pause at the end of phrases. You'll probably find that you'll have to slow down your pace quite a bit, as your normal rate of speaking will likely be much too fast for you to access the practice while also leading it. You'll want to use a warm tone, without sounding too sappy, since you want to be yourself. Don't worry about trying to sound like "The Best Teacher Delivering a Guided Practice." As I'm sure you know, teens can spot inauthenticity a mile away.

Ensuring a Trauma-Sensitive Practice

The students in your classroom may have experienced a wide range of traumas in their short lives, some that may have been life-threatening and others that may be considered more minor but still significant enough to result in fear and emotional pain. Of course, you don't want to inadvertently cause your students to revisit these traumatic events from their past without giving them tools to support themselves and teaching ways to navigate challenging emotions.

It is for this reason that trauma-sensitive precautions are foundational to this self-compassion curriculum and are embedded throughout. The following are some trauma-sensitive precautions that empower students by giving them choices and establishing a safe container:

1. Always invite students to participate, without requiring them to do so. In this way, students engage when they are ready. (*choice*)

2. During guided practices, give students the option of either closing their eyes or having a soft downward gaze. (*choice*)

3. Whenever possible, tell students ahead of time how long the practice will be and what it will involve. (*safe container*)

4. Allow students to opt out of the practice if they don't feel up to it that day. They can also stop the practice in the middle if they need. (*choice*)

5. Provide a grounding practice at the beginning of each session, even if it's just a minute or so. For example, you can ask students to notice the feeling of their feet on the floor or to notice sounds in the room. (*safe container*)

6. Provide a variety of practices for students to try out to see what works for them. There's no "one size fits all," and students can use the practices that work for them and let go of those that don't. (*choice*)

It may be helpful to remember that students don't have to take in all concepts and practices the first time through. Unlike other subjects you teach at school, self-compassion is a process of gradual unfolding that happens when students are ready. Think of it like planting a seed. You can't force it to grow. You can only plant the seed, which comes with its inherent ability to germinate, and tend to it as best you can. When the soil is fertile and conditions are right, it will take root and grow.

One final word about triggers and feelings of discomfort—self-compassion offers tools to deal with the emotional pain that arises from being human and alive. For this reason, it isn't always helpful to allow students to avoid difficult emotions or to jump in to fix their discomfort. As adults, our tendency is to smooth out bumps in the road so students don't have to stumble through. But it's only through stumbling that students will learn how to stand up again—taller this time—and take another step into the unavoidable and challenging territory of difficult emotions.

That means that in order for students to learn how to navigate through discomfort, they have to feel a *bit* of their pain and build their capacity for distress tolerance. Make sure to frequently remind students that they are always in charge of how much or how little they wish to engage with the practices. "Touching" the pain is okay (but accessing trauma is not).

CHAPTER 3

How to Conduct Inquiry in the Classroom

> **"** Listen to your life. See it for the fathomless mystery it is. In the boredom and pain of it, no less than in the excitement and gladness: touch, taste, smell your way to the holy and hidden heart of it, because in the last analysis all moments are key moments, and life itself is grace.
>
> **—Frederick Buechner**

Inquiry is a process through which students reflect on their inner experience of doing a guided self-compassion practice. Traditionally, this is a process that you will facilitate immediately after the completion of each practice, either through an exchange of dialogue or through student self-reflection. Either way, inquiry strengthens students' ability to be mindful and self-compassionate. It allows them to gain insight in one of two ways—(1) by seeing how they were already compassionate toward themselves in the practice, or (2) by identifying areas where they struggled in the practice and considering how self-compassion can be helpful in working through these struggles.

Know that inquiry in the classroom is different from inquiry in other venues, such as after-school programs. For one, students in the classroom know one another and may be more (or less, depending on the classroom dynamic) reluctant to share their personal experiences. Second, the group size in a classroom is usually larger than what you might have in an after-school program, which can make students less likely to share their feelings and be vulnerable. For these reasons, inquiry in the classroom requires a light touch. In this chapter, I'll discuss two different ways to approach inquiry in schools, depending on the size of the group, the setting, the age and maturity of the students, and the students' level of self-awareness.

Inquiry Option 1

When the class size is medium or large, or the environment doesn't lend itself to intimate or vulnerable conversation. In other words, a typical classroom.

In a typical classroom environment, you can conduct inquiry by asking students to respond to focused questions and to engage in reflective writing after each practice. Appendix 2 provides worksheets with accompanying inquiry questions that correspond to each session in the curriculum. Some of the questions are direct and require straightforward responses, such as "Were you able to feel your breath, even for a second?" Other questions require somewhat more introspection, such as "How does your body feel after the practice?" Each worksheet also contains a series of reflection questions that require more careful thought and are intended for older students or students who are more mature and able to think more deeply about their experience. It's best to use your judgment when deciding whether to assign the reflection questions.

Because many of the included worksheets ask students to reflect on their feelings in relation to the practice, an "emotion wheel" is provided on certain worksheets. Sometimes, students will have trouble articulating their emotions because they're not sure what they are feeling. Other times, they may have a sense of what they're feeling but aren't able to home in on it precisely. For example, they may be able to identify that they're feeling sad but struggle to identify more specific emotions like loneliness, hurt, or guilt. The emotion wheel can help them narrow down their experience. There are other emotion wheels available online that are geared to different age levels, depending on the needs of your students.

Remember that the purpose of the worksheets is to promote reflective thought about the student's experience. It is *not* meant as an assessment tool to see what they have learned. For this reason, students are given the option to respond to one or more questions and to draw or write about their experience. The worksheets are deliberately kept brief to accommodate the 45-to-50-minute-long class session. You may notice that some practices include both class discussion questions *and* related (or verbatim) inquiry questions on the accompanying worksheet. This is because some students will benefit from a discussion of their shared experience in class (helping them understand the common humanity component of self-compassion), while others will benefit from the self-reflection that the worksheets provide.

There's no need to collect the worksheets, as they are meant to be a tool for students, similar to a journal entry. If you do decide to collect the worksheets and comment on them, make sure to always validate each student's experience. Remember, there isn't one way to learn self-compassion, and each student's experience is valid and should not be judged.

Inquiry Option 2

> When the group is small and likely comfortable opening up to each other to some degree. A typical setting might be a group that is held in a school counselor's office.

In this type of setting, you facilitate inquiry by asking the small group a question that tracks each teen's experience of the practice. Suggested questions can be found in the inquiry sections of each practice within the curriculum section, but you don't have to feel tied to these specific questions. Younger students—middle schoolers, for example—respond better when you ask questions that are more specific. For example, in the *Compassionate Friend* practice, you might ask younger students, "Were you able to find a safe place? If so, what happened?" With older students who have a better developed ability to think abstractly, you can ask more open-ended questions, such as "What was that practice like for you? How did it make you feel?"

As you can imagine, this inquiry option is a bit more complex. It is a verbal exchange and a process in which you, as the counselor or teacher, are listening deeply to what each student is saying. This requires mindfulness on your part—an ability to stay present with the student without thinking of what to say next or getting distracted by something else going on in a corner of the room. (This is where having an assistant in the room comes in handy. They can respond to any distractions that arise.)

To listen deeply, you must be aware not only of the content the student is saying but also the feeling tone that is underlying the words. It is here that two-way communication, or *resonance*, takes place. You are not only hearing the student's words but also picking up on their feelings through their body language, subtle voice inflections, and nonverbal cues. When this kind of listening takes place, the student feels heard, or as the author, psychiatrist, and award-winning educator Dan Siegel (2010) says, the student "feels felt." And the student knows it. You can think of inquiry as 90 percent resonance (Germer & Neff, 2019).

Resonance is what happens when people really make an effort to listen and respond with interest and curiosity. It's a normal human encounter—in fact, it's the best kind of human encounter. Keep in mind that good teachers do this all the time. They are present with their students, can hear what their needs are (whether emotional or academic), and respond accordingly. Teachers are "need sleuths"—constantly having an ear out for what their students need. Granted, this can be hard to do when there are many needs coming at you all at once, but when it does happen, students feel heard.

How Do Teens Respond to Inquiry?

Students can respond to inquiry in a variety of ways. It's important to remember that learning in this way—talking about feelings, for example—is likely very new for them. And talking about feelings *in front of their peers* may be particularly scary and elicit feelings of vulnerability. For this reason, some students may respond by not responding at all.

But have no fear! In my experience teaching this program in a variety of contexts over the years, I have learned that it's best not to view students' lack of response as a reflection of your ability as a teacher (though this is an easy trap to fall into, and we all fall into it at times). It also doesn't mean that students aren't "getting it." In fact, I've heard from instructors who thought their students weren't learning because they hadn't said much during the program, only for the instructors to be amazed at the strikingly perceptive and insightful comments these students made at the end of the program. Remember that teens are struggling to figure out their way through a tangled mass of often overwhelming emotions, and they can be reluctant to share their feelings at this early and often precarious stage. Be careful not to misinterpret their lack of response for lack of engagement. Think of it like babies learning to speak—they spend a year or more listening to language before they begin to attempt to form words.

This is precisely why it is vital to create a safe container for your sessions. In a safe space, students are more likely to express themselves without fear of being harshly criticized or demeaned. They know that when they speak, others will listen. In order for students to be brave enough to be vulnerable, they need to feel a certain degree of safety and trust in the classroom environment.

When students do feel safe and ready to share what they experienced with a practice, they may do so for a number of reasons. One is that they simply want to share. They are seeking some kind of acknowledgment for their experience. (You know this student—they're the one with their hand up all the time!) Another reason is that they are somewhat troubled by what they experienced during the practice, and they need some help figuring it out. Let's envision a couple of different ways this might play out.

For example, after the *Compassionate Friend* practice, you might ask, "When you did this practice, were you able to find a safe space? If so, what was it like to be in this space?" (Visualizing a "safe space" is the first part of the practice.) In response, Diego raises his hand and says, "Yes, I sure did! It was an awesome place that was kind of like out of a video game. There were all these wild, overgrown paths and woods, and so many fun places to go!" Diego's response falls in the first category—he wanted to share the cool place that came up for him in his mind. You can respond with a simple "Thank you!" and that's it—inquiry with Diego is done!

Next, Kaya raises her hand and says, "Nothing happened for me. I couldn't find a safe place at all. It was all like a blank screen." Kaya might be somewhat upset by her inability to come up with a safe place, but it may be that she's okay with it as well. Your next step would be to check in with her and see how she feels about it. You might ask, "Kaya, how was that for you? Not being able to find a safe place?" She might either respond with "I'm okay with it" or "It kind of bothered me that I couldn't come up with anything." If she's okay with not being able to come up with a safe place, you can simply thank her for her response and move on. But if she's upset by it—*aha!*—here's where you remember the intention of inquiry: to help her build her self-compassion muscle.

First, you can help her track her experience by asking, "What did you do when you noticed that you were bothered because you couldn't find a safe place?" Perhaps Kaya responds with "I kept trying and felt worse and worse." At this point, you might check in with her to see if she's still upset by asking, "How are you feeling right now?" If Kaya indicates that she is still upset, make sure to validate her feelings, perhaps by reflecting back to her something like "I can see you're upset." This way, Kaya knows she has been heard.

Next, you can ask her what she feels like she needs right now. Often, students are able to articulate *something* about their needs. Maybe simply being heard is enough for them to feel better. If Kaya becomes stuck and can't communicate what she needs, you can gently guide her to use any self-compassion tools that she has learned so far. You might say, "Can you think of any words you could say to support yourself simply because you're feeling bad? Perhaps some words that you might say to a friend who was feeling similarly?" If she remains stuck, you can either suggest a few phrases ("Oh, I'm so sorry you're feeling this way. I know this is really hard.") or perhaps suggest a different self-compassion tool ("Can you use one of your supportive gestures to support yourself?").

Another option—and I'd only suggest doing this if you are confident that there's a feeling of trust within the group—is to bring the conversation out to the group, asking whether anyone has any ideas of ways to support themselves in this type of situation. However, if you sense that Kaya is feeling uncomfortable or vulnerable, it's important to take the spotlight off her and not use this approach.

Inquiry with each student should take no more than two or three minutes. In general, and often this is dependent on how much time you have, you'd conduct inquiry with two or three students in each postpractice inquiry session, for a total inquiry time of four to nine minutes. Remember that all the students in the group are observing and learning from the inquiry interaction that is taking place, so no need to conduct inquiry with more than two or three.

A few helpful hints when doing inquiry:

- The value of validating a student's feeling cannot be overstated. The knowledge that you have been seen and heard is a foundational need of all humans, and it is a gift that you can offer your students.

- Trust yourself on when to end inquiry. If there is no conflict in what a student is sharing, or the conflict has been resolved, there is no need to extend the inquiry further. You can simply thank them for sharing and end the inquiry. If you're unsure, you can check in with the student and ask, "Are you okay now?"

- If you sense that a student may be uncomfortable sharing, ask permission to continue ("Is it okay if I ask another question?"). It's important to recognize the power differential that exists between teachers and students, which could result in a student's desire to please you. Therefore, it's important to follow up by reassuring the student that it's completely okay if they want to discontinue inquiry ("It's totally okay to say no, by the way. And I mean that!").

- Be aware of your own striving to be a good self-compassion teacher and inquirer. We all want to be good at what we do, especially when it comes to helping students. That's natural, particularly with teachers who have big hearts and are committed to helping students alleviate their emotional pain. But when it comes to learning self-compassion, it's okay—even encouraged—to be a slow learner. So be patient and kind to yourself!

When you engage in inquiry, it's important to keep its overarching purpose in the back of your mind—to strengthen the resources of mindfulness and self-compassion. You'll recall that mindfulness is about being aware of your experiences without getting carried away by them or avoiding them altogether. It allows you to sit with difficult experiences with a clear perspective and without the pull of emotion-laden thoughts. Then, self-compassion steps in and allows you to respond to those difficult experiences with kindness and support.

In this way, mindfulness is the foundation of self-compassion. You need to be mindfully aware of your feelings and experiences in order to support yourself with self-compassion. You need to know *when* and *where* you're experiencing distress in order to step in with self-compassion. In this way, the practice of mindfulness undergirds and supports the practice of self-compassion.

With this goal in mind, you want to promote student self-reflection so students can call on their newly learned self-compassion tools when they are feeling discomfort, stress, or emotional pain. When they can articulate their emotions with greater subtlety and nuance, they are better able to know what they need and therefore more able to meet those needs with self-compassion.

Ready to dive into the curriculum? Here we go!

PART 2

The Curriculum

CHAPTER 4

The 16-Session Curriculum

> " I have been trying recently to wake up in the morning and give myself some sort of deliberately kind start—to consciously and intentionally take the first self-denigrating or negatively tinged thought that arrives in my head and slide it off to one side. Then I invite a second thought, a better and more tender one, something more intentional, more friendly to self. And I choose that as my launching point. Often, it's just a quiet but grateful acknowledgment that I have made it once again to the starting line of a new day.
>
> **—Michelle Obama**

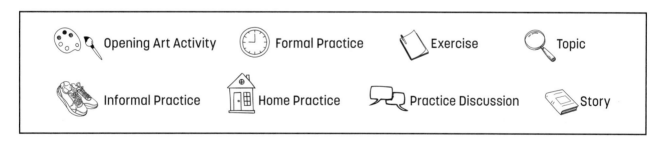

Session 1: Discovering Mindful Self-Compassion

Opening Art Activity: Mindful Drawing Squiggles (10 min)

Formal Practice: Sunbathing (8 min)

Exercise: Community Agreements (10 min)

Topic: What Is Mindful Self-Compassion? (5 min)

Formal Practice: Compassionate Friend (10 min)

Home Practice (2 min)

Session 2: Being Kind to Myself

Opening Art Activity: Drawing My Safe Place, Part 1 (10 min)

Practice Discussion (5 min)

Exercise: How Would I Treat a Friend? (25 min)

Informal Practice: Supportive Gestures (10 min)

Home Practice (2 min)

Session 3: Paying Attention on Purpose

Opening Art Activity: Drawing My Safe Place, Part 2 (10 min)

Informal Practice: Sound Practice (10 min)

Topic: What Is Mindfulness? (10 min)

Informal Practice: Soles of the Feet (10 min)

Home Practice (2 min)

Session 4: Mindfulness

Opening Art Activity: Here-and-Now Stone Drawing (10 min)

Informal Practice: Mindful Eating (10 min)

Formal Practice: Compassionate Body Scan (15 min)

Topic: Wandering Mind (5 min)

Informal Practice: Here-and-Now Stone (5 min)

Home Practice (2 min)

Session 5: The Adolescent Brain

Opening Art Activity: Mindful Brain Coloring (10 min)

Topic: When Self-Compassion Can Be Difficult (5 min)

Topic: The Developing Teen Brain (15 min)

Formal Practice: Affectionate Breathing (10 min)

Informal Practice: Three Soothing Breaths (3 min)

Home Practice (2 min)

Session 6: Kindness

Opening Art Activity: Kindness Phrases (10 min)

Formal Practice: Kindness for Someone You Care About (15 min)

Topic: Practicing with Kindness Phrases (5 min)

Informal Practice: Finding Kindness Phrases (15 min)

Home Practice (2 min)

Session 7: Laying the Foundation for Self-Compassion

Opening Art Activity: First Initial (10 min)

Formal Practice: A Person Just Like Me (10 min)

Practice Discussion (10 min)

Formal Practice: Calming Music (10 min)

Home Practice (2 min)

Session 8: Self-Compassion

Opening Art Activity: Drawing to Music (10 min)

Topic: Self-Compassion (5 min)

Topic: Self-Criticism and Safety (5 min)

Exercise: Motivating Ourselves with Compassion (20 min)

Home Practice (2 min)

Session 9: Self-Compassion vs. Self-Esteem

Opening Art Activity: Mindful Drawing to Music (10 min)

Topic: Self-Esteem vs. Self-Compassion (10 min)

Exercise: The Cost of Social Comparison (15 min)

Exercise: Social Media Exploration (10 min)

Home Practice (2 min)

Session 10: Common Humanity

Opening Art Activity: Japanese Bowl (10 min)

Practice Discussion (5 min)

Exercise: Crossing the Line (10 min)

Exercise: Japanese Bowls (15 min)

Story: A Cracked Pot (while completing the *Japanese Bowls* exercise)

Home Practice (2 min)

Session 11: Core Values

Opening Art Activity: Mindful Frame (10 min)

Topic: Core Values (5 min)

Exercise: My House/My Self (25 min)

Home Practice (2 min)

Session 12: Silver Linings

Opening Art Activity: A Pledge to Myself (10 min)

Formal Practice: Giving and Receiving Compassion (15 min)

Topic: Finding Value in Our Struggles (5 min)

Exercise: Silver Linings (15 min)

Home Practice (2 min)

Session 13: Getting to Know Difficult Emotions

Opening Art Activity: Oobleck (15 min)

Formal Practice: Noticing Sounds (10 min)

Topic: Working with Difficult Emotions (5 min)

Informal Practice: Soften, Support, Open (15 min)

Home Practice (2 min)

Session 14: Anger and the Adolescent Brain

Opening Art Activity: Egg Writing (10 min)

Practice Discussion (5 min)

Topic: The Adolescent Brain (10 min)

Topic: Working with Anger (5 min)

Informal Practice: Exploring Unmet Needs (15 min)

Home Practice (2 min)

Session 15: Embracing Your Life with Gratitude

Opening Art Activity: Things That Make You Smile (10 min)

Topic: Negativity Bias (5 min)

Formal Practice: Calming Music (10 min)

Topic: Gratitude (10 min)

Exercise: Finding Gratitude (10 min)

Home Practice (2 min)

Session 16: Maintaining the Practice

Opening Art Activity: Creating Writing Paper (10 min)

Formal Practice: Compassionate Friend (10 min)

Topic: Self-Appreciation (5 min)

Exercise: What Would I Like to Remember? (15 min)

Closing: Sharing Thoughts (5 min)

 **SESSION 1**

Discovering Mindful Self-Compassion

Session Overview

- *Opening Art Activity*: Mindful Drawing Squiggles (10 min)
- *Formal Practice*: Sunbathing (8 min)
- *Exercise*: Community Agreements (10 min)
- *Topic*: What Is Mindful Self-Compassion? (5 min)
- *Formal Practice*: Compassionate Friend (10 min)
- *Home Practice* (2 min)

In This Session, You Will . . .

- Orient students to the program
- Increase awareness of their capacity for self-compassion

Materials

- Paper
- Colored pencils

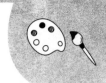

Mindful Drawing Squiggles

10 minutes

Intention

- Help teens transition from their regular class to self-compassion class by stilling and quieting the mind

Instructions

- Ask students to draw a lengthy one-line "squiggle" on an 8½" × 11" piece of paper. For example:

- When students are done squiggling, have them take time to color in the closed spaces however they would like with colored pencils (not crayons or markers) and decorate the outside spaces as well.

FORMAL PRACTICE

Sunbathing

5 minutes (practice)
3 minutes (inquiry)

Intention

- Help students settle and transition from other classes

- Provide an example of how visualization can help us relax

Instructions

- Read the following script to students:

Relax into a comfortable sitting position. If you're comfortable closing your eyes, feel free to do that. If not, you can keep your eyes at a downward gaze so you're not distracted by things around you. Take a few breaths to simply allow yourself to settle and relax. With each exhale, let go of stress and tension in your body, letting go a little more with each exhale.

Next, imagine you're on a beautiful, exotic beach. In front of you is the ocean—a deep green-blue color, against the cloudless light blue sky. You lie down on the sand and feel the sun on your skin. You can feel your skin soaking up the warmth of the sun, almost like a sponge. The warmth is perfect—not too hot, just enough so that it feels just right against your skin. In fact, it's just what you need right now.

As you lie here, you notice that there seems to be a feeling coming with the warmth, a feeling that envelops you, holds you, supports you. It's a feeling of overwhelming calmness, a knowingness, a sense of peace. And you hear (or feel, or simply know) some words: "Everything is going to be okay." Somehow, deep in your bones, you know this to be true. You know that whatever happens, however things work out, all will be okay.

You lie on the sand, feeling the warmth of the sun permeating your body, offering you a deep sense of peace, of unconditional acceptance, and an inner knowledge that all will be well.

You can stay here for as long as you like. And when you're ready, gently open your eyes.

Inquiry

- What did it feel like to imagine having the sun on your face?

- What was it like when I said, "Everything is going to be okay"?

- Did you notice anything else? Remember, there are no wrong answers. There is no right or wrong way to feel. All answers are welcome!

Community Agreements

10 minutes

Intention

- Create a cooperative climate and get students to "buy in" to the program

Instructions

- Explain to students that this is a different kind of class from their normal classes. Ask students:

    ○ "What do you need to feel safe in here? To be able to open up and talk comfortably and feel like you're being heard?"

    ○ "What would allow you to feel comfortable and encourage participation in a group of peers?"

- Brainstorm a list of "community agreements" that will make this a safe and comfortable space. Make sure students include the following guidelines in the list: maintaining confidentiality, no advice giving, respecting each other, and listening deeply.

- Encourage student participation by asking a group member to write down the list of agreements on the whiteboard as students brainstorm. Keep it for later reference.

- Emphasize the principles of *curiosity* and *openness*. Explain that regardless of whose idea it was for students to be in this class, they should treat it like an experiment. See what happens.

- Go over the guidelines for mindful sharing:

    ○ Speak what is true for you, not what you think might be true for others.

    ○ Hold off on telling long stories that others may not be able to relate to.

    ○ As you're speaking, notice what you're feeling.

    ○ Listen deeply.

- If you are an extrovert and enjoy sharing, please remember that others might need a little more time to think about what they want to say before sharing. Please make room for everyone.
- Ask for clarification when needed.

Diversity

- It is important to acknowledge diversity in the room and how it may impact a student's experience of the course. The issue of diversity below may have already been discussed to some extent in your classroom. If so, feel free to just lightly revisit the following talking points. If not, it is important that you go over this topic.

- Explain to students that respect is about honoring the differences between us. It's about respecting diversity. Common sources of individual difference are race, ethnicity, religion, gender, sexuality, neurodiversity, abilities, age, social class, health, nationality, and body type. Likewise, as everyone's brains develop slightly differently and at different rates, no two brains function alike.

- Most importantly, there may be more diversity than meets the eye. For example, some teens are questioning their sexuality and/or gender, and often this is not apparent. Others may be struggling with a chronic health issue.

- It is important to emphasize that everyone is welcome here in this space and that we want to hear from everyone. Diversity brings richness of experience, meaning that diversity of all kinds will make this class better.

What Is Mindful Self-Compassion?

5 minutes

Intention

- Offer a conceptual understanding of what the next 16 sessions will be about

- Provide brief definitions of mindfulness and self-compassion, including how the two concepts are related

- Provide an opportunity for students to engage in an interactive discussion

Talking Points

- Ask students to describe what they believe mindfulness and self-compassion are:

  There are two components to this class—mindfulness and self-compassion. What is mindfulness? Have you heard of this before? [Accept all answers, adding clarification if necessary.] *What do you think self-compassion is?* [Discuss.]

- Provide definitions of mindfulness and self-compassion. Keep the definitions very brief. There will be a lot of time to expand later in the curriculum. You don't want to overload students with too much conceptual information now!

  Mindfulness is about being aware of what is happening in the present moment with curiosity and with a sense of openness. Self-compassion involves meeting that feeling or experience with kindness, courage, and strength, particularly in times of struggle and difficulty. This also includes protecting ourselves from harmful situations and people, making efforts to meet our own needs, and standing up for ourselves when necessary.

  This class is about sitting down, noticing our feelings, and offering ourselves what we need. This is a class where we will learn to be nicer to ourselves and take care of ourselves. We all say harsh things to ourselves sometimes, so this class will teach us to become aware of those times and then choose a kinder and healthier way of being with ourselves.

Teaching Tip: The advantage of breaking into small groups for this discussion is that students will feel less pressured to speak than they would in a large group. Please use your judgment as to what might be the best format to use for your group, knowing that breaking into small groups takes a bit more time. If you break into small groups, it's important to come back to the large group to clarify definitions.

FORMAL PRACTICE

Compassionate Friend

5 minutes (practice)
5 minutes (inquiry)

Intention

- Show teens that they have a compassionate voice within themselves

- Help teens understand that they are capable of directing this compassionate voice toward themselves

Instructions

- Read the following script to students:

Begin by taking a few deep inhalations, allowing your shoulders to relax away from your ears. If you'd like to fold your arms and put your head down on your desk, feel free to do that. You can close your eyes if that's okay with you. It's often easier to use your imagination with your eyes closed.

Take a few moments to allow yourself to imagine a place where you feel safe, comfortable, and relaxed. This can be a real or imagined place, but somewhere that allows you to breathe comfortably and let go of any worry. Perhaps this place is in nature—a beach or an opening in the woods near a brook—or maybe it's a corner of your bedroom or the comfort of a good friend's house. It might even be an imaginary place, like a cloud. Imagine this place in as much detail as you can, including what you hear, smell, and (most of all) feel like in this place.

Soon you'll receive a visitor—a warm and kind friend. This is someone who loves you completely and accepts you exactly for who you are. This can be a real person, like a friend of yours, a beloved grandparent, or a favorite teacher, or it can be a character from a book you've read, a pet, or even a superhero from a video game, comic book, or movie. It can also be some being that you create from your imagination. Imagine this being in as much detail as possible, especially how it feels to be in their presence.

Your compassionate friend cares deeply about you and just wants you to be happy. Soon you will be greeting this compassionate friend. You have a choice—you can either go out from your safe place to meet your friend, or you can invite them in. Imagine that you are doing that now, allowing yourself to sit with the person at just the right distance, feeling completely comfortable and safe, completely accepted and loved.

Take a moment to enjoy how you feel in the presence of your compassionate friend.

This person or being is here with you now and can understand exactly what it's like to be you. They know exactly where you are in your life right now and understand precisely what you are struggling with.

And this person or being accepts and understands you completely for who you are, perhaps better than anyone else.

This being has something important to say to you, something that is just what you need to hear right now. See if you can listen closely for the words they want to share, words that are comforting and supportive.

And if no words come, that's okay too. Just enjoy being in the presence of your compassionate friend.

And now, maybe you have something to say to this friend. This friend is a very good listener and completely understands you. Is there anything you'd like to say?

Enjoy your friend's good company for a few last moments, and wave goodbye to your friend, knowing that you can invite them back whenever you need to. You are now alone in your safe place again. Let yourself savor what just happened, perhaps reflecting on the words you heard.

Before this practice ends, please remember that this compassionate friend is a part of you. The presence you felt and the words you heard are a deep part of yourself. The comfort and safety that you may be feeling is there within you at all times. Know that you can return to this safe place and to this compassionate friend whenever you need to.

Bringing your attention back to your breath, gently open your eyes if they've been closed.

Inquiry

- Were you able to find a place that felt safe and comfortable?

- Were you able to identify a compassionate friend?

- What is it like to know that you have this compassionate friend inside you at all times?

Teaching Tip: There are some teens who will not be able to think of a compassionate and understanding person in their life. For this reason, it is important to give them the option of creating an imaginary person. Make sure to include this option when conducting this guided practice.

HOME PRACTICE

2 minutes

Intention

- Set expectations for practice outside of each session

- Provide an opportunity for students to reinforce their learning by verbalizing what they are going to "take with" them from the session

Instructions

- Emphasize that this is *not* homework, but an opportunity to practice being kind to themselves. Encourage each student to be their own scientist, with each practice serving as their laboratory.

- Encourage them to make the practice playful and easy. Remind them that this is a way for them to be kind and nurturing to themselves.

- As much as possible, encourage them to let go of striving, perfectionism, or the desire to "do it right." Instead, be open to the experience and to experimentation.

- Discuss where students can access the recordings of the guided practices and the class materials. A list of recordings is available at https://karenbluth .com/msct-in-schools (or use the QR code provided here).

- Explain that these practices are now a part of students' toolkits. They can try them out and see which ones work best for them. As you continue with the curriculum, they will continue adding practices to their toolkit.

- New tools for the toolkit: *Sunbathing*; *Compassionate Friend*

Toolkit	
Informal Tools	**Formal Tools**
	1. Sunbathing
	2. Compassionate Friend

Wrap-Up

- What will you take away from this session? [*Ask for a volunteer to start, and then go around the room, with each student offering something that stands out to them about this session. Give students the option to pass if they do not want to share. If time is limited, ask just a few students to respond.*]

 **SESSION 2**

Being Kind to Myself

Session Overview

- *Opening Art Activity*: Drawing My Safe Place, Part 1 (10 min)

- *Practice Discussion* (5 min)

- *Exercise*: How Would I Treat a Friend? (25 min)

- *Informal Practice*: Supportive Gestures (10 min)

- *Home Practice* (2 min)

In This Session, You Will . . .

- Articulate the definition of self-compassion

- Teach students several self-compassion tools

Materials

- Colored pencils

- White paper

- List of challenging situations cut up and placed in an envelope

- Sheets of paper that say "How I would treat myself" on one side and "How I would treat a friend" on the other side (*optional*)

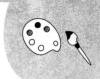

Drawing My Safe Place, Part 1

10 minutes

Intention

- Help teens transition from their regular class to self-compassion class by stilling and quieting the mind

- Allow students to articulate, imagine, and internalize their "safe place"

- Help students create community and connection

Instructions

- Encourage students to use colored pencils to draw their safe place or to convey the feeling they have in their safe place. For students who are more literal, drawing the place itself will work, while for other students, it might be more helpful to simply express the feeling that they have in this place. In other words, all representations are accepted—either a literal expression of their place (a drawing of a special place in the woods, for example) or simply an abstract array of color. They will be working on this art activity during this session, as well as in the following session.

5 minutes

Intention

- Check in with students about how their practice has been going since the last session

- Make sure students have all been able to access the audio recordings and class materials

Instructions

- When checking in with students, it's important to gently encourage them to practice, but not to admonish them *at all* if they haven't. Admonishing, scolding, or (worse) shaming them for not practicing will only cause more resistance. Here are some ways you can gently encourage them to practice:

Has anyone experienced any stress since the last session? [Most students will have experienced some stress. Asking the question in this way allows them to learn that stress is an opening to practice self-compassion.]

Did you try the Sunbathing *practice? How about the* Compassionate Friend *practice? What was it like? How did you feel afterward?* [Make sure students were able to access the recordings.]

Research shows that the more we practice, the more we benefit. Of course, it's completely up to you how much you practice—or if you practice at all. But know that the more you practice, the more you will benefit. Research also has shown that short, "informal" practices—those that we do in the moment when we're feeling stressed or upset—are effective. We'll be learning an informal practice today. So don't forget about those!

Remember that home practice is not homework, but a time when we can get away from all the stress of school, chores, or whatever is happening in our social lives that might be stressful and simply take care of ourselves. It's a time to soothe ourselves, to relax a little, and just to rest. We'll be learning lots of other ways to do this in the upcoming sessions.

How Would I Treat a Friend?

15 minutes (exercise)
10 minutes (discussion)

Intention

- Help teens to see how they tend to treat others more kindly than they treat themselves

Instructions

- Separate the class into small groups of four or five and have each group select a challenging situation from the envelope:

    o Received a bad grade on an important test or paper

    o Boy/girlfriend broke up with them

    o Got into a fight with parent and said things they later regretted

    o Felt bad about themselves because they didn't get invited to an event that everyone else was invited to

    o Didn't make the team

    o Missed an important goal in a soccer game

    o Stressed about workload and worried that GPA will drop

    o Dropped new phone and the screen shattered

    o Got ACT/SAT scores back and didn't do as well as expected

    o Found out that their crush asked someone else out

- After each group selects a situation, give them the following instructions:

    Close your eyes and notice what you are feeling inside. Take a moment to ask yourself how you would treat a friend in this situation.

- Give each student a piece of paper, then ask them to draw or write about how they would treat a friend if this situation happened to them.

- After about five minutes, ask students to close their eyes as you give them the following instructions:

    Now close your eyes again and imagine that this situation has happened to you. Imagine that you were the one who didn't make the team, for example. What are the words that you would say to yourself if this happened to you? As you think of how you would treat yourself, be aware of your thoughts (e.g., "I should have been more careful! I'm so stupid!"), feelings (e.g., anger, frustration, sadness), and sensations (e.g., chest tightness, sweaty palms, rapid heartbeat) that you have.

- Now instruct teens to take five minutes in their small groups to flip the paper over and write or draw how they would treat themselves if they were experiencing this situation.

- After five minutes, have all students return to the full group.

- Then ask teens to share their responses on how they would treat a friend and write these responses on the whiteboard, categorizing their responses into the three different components of self-compassion. For example, "You're a really great friend. I'm here for you" (*kindness*), "Are you okay? I promise you're not going to feel this way forever" (*mindfulness*), and "I know how you feel, this happened to me last week" (*common humanity*). It is helpful to write the three components in different colors. You will explain the three different categories in a few minutes.

- Next, ask students to share their responses to how they would treat themselves, and write this on the whiteboard, inquiring if they see differences in how they treat themselves versus how they treat their good friends. (Students will say they are much harder on themselves than on their friends.) It is helpful to explain to students that self-compassion is difficult for all people, not just teens, and preliminary research indicates that about 80 percent of people are significantly more compassionate to others than they are to themselves (Knox & Neff, 2016).

- Explain that the informal definition of self-compassion is treating ourselves with the same kindness and support as we treat our good friends.

- Now explain that there is a formal definition of self-compassion, which encompasses three components (refer to the three categories you created earlier on the whiteboard):

    o **Self-kindness** (vs. self-judgment): Treating ourselves with the same kindness, support, and love that we would give a good friend

    o **Mindfulness** (vs. catastrophizing or overidentification): Not getting caught up in the drama, but not avoiding our pain either—being able to be with feelings as they are

- ○ **Common humanity** (vs. isolation): Knowing that others experience the same feelings as we do and that these feelings are part of growing up—everyone suffers

---

Teaching Tip: Ahead of time, consider folding sheets of paper down the middle so that one side says, "How I would treat a friend," and the other side says, "How I would treat myself." Hand them to students with the "How I would treat a friend" side face up.

Discussion

- What did you learn about yourself in this exercise?

- What were the differences in how you treated a friend versus how you treated yourself?

- What was it like to realize that?

Supportive Gestures

5 minutes (practice)
5 minutes (discussion)

Intention

- Guide teens in finding ways to give themselves physical self-compassion

Instructions

- Many teens have developed self-soothing strategies that help them cope in the moment but that are unhealthy or even harmful in the long run. By adding healthy coping strategies to their toolkit, they can calm and comfort the nervous system in more effective ways.

- Explain to students that our bodies respond to self-soothing practices more quickly than our minds. There is a physiological reason for this. When we make physical contact through a soothing gesture, either with ourselves or with others (e.g., by giving a friend a hug), a hormone called oxytocin is released. This hormone, commonly called the "feel-good chemical," can elicit feelings of trust and relaxation and reduce the stress response.

- Remind students that we readily use comforting gestures with our friends when they are feeling badly. We think nothing of giving them a hug, putting an arm around them, or patting them on the shoulder or back. But we don't do these gestures for ourselves—only because we haven't been raised to do them. But we can learn!

- Explain the current practice:

  We're going to try out a few supportive gestures to see if we can find one or two that feel comforting and supportive. You can close your eyes if you're comfortable doing so, because sometimes it's easier to get in touch with what you feel when your eyes are closed. Of course, it's totally fine to keep your eyes open as well.

- Then guide students through the following gestures, spending 10 to 15 seconds on each gesture. As you do so, periodically remind them to notice what they're feeling

with each gesture. For example, they might notice the warmth and gentle pressure of their hand on their heart or the coolness of their hand on their cheek.

- o Rubbing two hands together
- o Crossing your arms and stroking your upper arms
- o Crossing your arms and giving yourself a gentle squeeze
- o Stroking your cheek
- o Cradling your face in your hands and leaning on a table
- o Placing one or two hands over your heart
- o Gently rubbing your chest using circular movements
- o Placing one hand on your abdomen
- o Placing one hand on your abdomen and one over your heart
- o Cupping one hand with your other hand as both hands rest in your lap
- o Placing one hand on your forehead and the other on the back of your neck
- o Placing one hand in a fist over your chest, with the other hand holding the wrist of the first hand

Discussion

- Were you able to find a gesture that felt comforting or soothing?
- Can you imagine a time when you would use this? If so, when?

Teaching Tip: Most teens will be able to find a gesture or two that feels supportive to them. If they aren't able to find any, you might ask if they have a gesture they already use. You can also explain that they have plenty of time to explore and try out different gestures. Finally, remind them that not every practice will be right for everyone. This program is about offering an array of different practices, so students can pick and choose those they like and want to incorporate into their daily lives.

HOME PRACTICE

2 minutes

Intention

- Reinforce skills learned in the session

Instructions

- Explain the difference between formal and informal practices. Formal practice involves setting aside time each day to practice (anywhere from 5 to 15 minutes or longer), while informal practice involves practicing when something stressful comes up. With informal practice, you take a few moments right then and there to practice.

- Encourage students to practice 5 to 10 minutes of formal practice per day, either with *Sunbathing* or *Compassionate Friend*, in addition to practicing informally with *Supportive Gestures* throughout the week. When they're struggling, also encourage them to ask themselves, "How would I treat a friend in this situation? Can I treat myself with the same kindness and support?"

- Remind students to make the home practice fun and easy. It is a way for them to be kind to themselves. It is not homework!

- New tools for the toolkit: *Supportive Gestures; Good Friend Question*

Toolkit	
Informal Tools	**Formal Tools**
1. Supportive Gestures	1. Sunbathing
2. Good Friend Question (Ask yourself: How would I treat a friend?)	2. Compassionate Friend

Wrap-Up

- What will you take away from this session? [*Ask for a volunteer to start, and then go around the room, with each student offering something that stands out to them about this session. Give students the option to pass if they do not want to share. If time is limited, ask just a few students to respond.*]

 **SESSION 3**

Paying Attention on Purpose

Session Overview

- *Opening Art Activity*: Drawing My Safe Place, Part 2 (10 min)

- *Informal Practice*: Sound Practice (10 min)

- *Topic*: What Is Mindfulness? (10 min)

- *Informal Practice*: Soles of the Feet (10 min)

- *Home Practice* (2 min)

In This Session, You Will . . .

- Explore the definition of mindfulness and help students experience mindful awareness

- Bring mindful awareness to the present-moment experience

- Calm the mind by anchoring attention on a single object or focal point

Materials

- Colored pencils and regular pencils

- Bell or chime (avoid using anything that may be interpreted as a religious object, such as a Tibetan singing bowl)

- YouTube video: "Mindfulness: Youth Voices" (https://www.youtube.com /watch?v=kk7IBwuhXWM)

Drawing My Safe Place, Part 2

10 minutes

Intention

- Help students transition from their regular class to self-compassion class by stilling and quieting the mind

- Allow them to articulate, imagine, and internalize their "safe place"

- Help teens create community and connection

Instructions

- Ask students to continue drawing or expressing the safe place that they started in the last session.

- Suggest that they take a moment to reflect on what might make them feel particularly safe in this place. They can bring in personal items to their safe place, such as books, photos, special mementos, or pets.

Sound Practice

10 minutes

Intention

- Introduce the sense of hearing as a way to practice mindfulness

Instructions

- Have students take a moment to settle into their chairs. Don't give them a warning that you will be ringing a bell.

- Ring the bell, then ask students what they heard. (Accept all answers.)

- Explain to students that you are going to ring the bell a second time and instruct them to pay careful attention to what they hear.

- Ring the bell a second time, then ask students what they heard this time. (Accept all answers.) Ask if they heard more the first or second time and why. Generally, teens will hear more the second time because they had instructions to pay attention. Clarify that when they make the intention to pay attention, they take in more information.

- Now ask students to take a few minutes to listen to the sounds around them. Offer one minute of silence and listening.

- After one minute, ask students what they heard. Did they notice more now? Explain that sounds are always around them. Again, make sure that students understand that when they have the intention to pay attention, they hear and see much more.

- Explain that paying attention to sound is a mindfulness practice—a way to anchor attention to the present moment, to what's happening at any given time.

- As an introduction to what will be coming, ask students if their minds wandered at any point during the practice. Assure them that everyone's mind will naturally wander and that you will be talking more about the wandering mind at a later point.

What Is Mindfulness?

10 minutes

Intention

- Review the understanding of what this mindful self-compassion course is about

- Provide a conceptual understanding of mindfulness

Talking Points

- From our previous discussion in class, remember that this is a class on mindful self-compassion. Who remembers what that is?

- How would you define mindfulness?

- Mindfulness is the foundation of mindful self-compassion. Mindfulness allows us to be aware when we are struggling, and it's necessary for us to recognize when this happens so we can respond to ourselves with support and kindness.

- One definition of mindfulness that is commonly used is "the awareness that arises through paying attention, on purpose, in the present moment, non-judgmentally" (Kabat-Zinn, 1994, p. 4).

- [*Show students "Mindfulness: Youth Voices" (https://www.youtube.com/watch?v=kk7lBwuhXWM)*]

- Discussion (*optional*): Has anyone here ever felt what the teens in this video felt? For example, feeling overwhelmed? Worried about the future? What was that like? Mindfulness gives us tools to work with those feelings.

Soles of the Feet*

5 minutes (practice)
5 minutes (discussion)

Intention

- Provide a direct experience of mindful awareness

- Introduce students to an easy and effective way to calm the mind when they're feeling overwhelmed with thoughts and emotions

Instructions

- Ask students to stand up and feel the soles of their feet on the floor. Then read through the following script, pausing about 10 seconds after each instruction:

Notice the sensation of your feet on the floor, maybe noticing the hardness or softness of the floor. Is there some cushiony feeling beneath your feet? Or does it feel hard?

Now lean forward just a half inch. What changes do you notice on the bottoms of your feet?

Now lean backward just a half inch. Notice what's happening on the bottoms of your feet.

Leaning to your left just a tiny bit, notice what's going on at the bottoms of your feet.

Now lean to your right. Notice any changes that are happening on the bottoms of your feet.

If, at any time, you notice that your mind has wandered and you're no longer noticing the feeling of your feet on the floor, simply guide your attention back to the sensations on the soles of your feet, remembering that mind wandering doesn't mean you're doing anything wrong. That is what minds naturally do.

Rock forward and backward a little, then side to side, just paying attention to the changing sensations in the soles of your feet.

Now bend your knees slightly, and make slow, small circles with your knees, noticing what's happening on the bottoms of your feet as you do this.

Now circle your knees in the opposite direction.

Notice how these two small surface areas of the feet support your entire body all day long. Perhaps offer a moment of appreciation or gratitude for all the hard work that your feet do for you.

---

* Adapted from Felver & Singh (2020).

Now come back to center, noticing how your feet feel as you are standing here.

You can return to your seat.

Discussion

- What did you notice when you anchored your attention in your feet? [*Make sure to accept all answers and acknowledge that students were being mindful when they noticed their experience.*]

- Were you able to give just a little appreciation to your feet?

Teaching Tip: Remind teens that this is a practice they can do at any time when they are beginning to feel stressed or upset. They do not have to be standing to do it but can even do it sitting in their seats. No one will even know!

HOME PRACTICE

2 minutes

Intention

- Reinforce skills learned in the session

Instructions

- Encourage students to practice 5 to 10 minutes of formal practice per day from the toolkit, in addition to practicing informally throughout the week with the new practices of *Soles of the Feet* and *Sound Practice*. For reinforcement, they can also continue using *Supportive Gestures* and asking themselves how they would treat a friend when they feel stressed, upset, or anxious.

- New tools for the toolkit: *Sound Practice*; *Soles of the Feet*

Toolkit	
Informal Tools	**Formal Tools**
1. Supportive Gestures	1. Sunbathing
2. Good Friend Question (Ask yourself: How would I treat a friend?)	2. Compassionate Friend
3. Sound Practice	
4. Soles of the Feet	

Wrap-Up

- What will you take away from this session? [*Ask for a volunteer to start, and then go around the room, with each student offering something that stands out to them about this session. Give students the option to pass if they do not want to share. If time is limited, ask just a few students to respond.*]

 **SESSION 4**

Mindfulness

Session Overview

- *Opening Art Activity*: Here-and-Now Stone Drawing (10 min)
- *Informal Practice*: Mindful Eating (10 min)
- *Formal Practice*: Compassionate Body Scan (15 min)
- *Topic*: Wandering Mind (5 min)
- *Informal Practice*: Here-and-Now Stone (5 min)
- *Home Practice* (2 min)

In This Session, You Will . . .

- Continue exploring mindfulness
- Bring mindful awareness to the present-moment experience
- Expand on how mindfulness activities can alleviate anxiety and stress

Materials

- Dried cranberries, raisins, or other small fruit (e.g., a mandarin orange, grapes)
- White paper
- Pencils
- Bag of small, polished stones

Here-and-Now Stone Drawing

10 minutes

Intention

- Help students transition from their regular class to self-compassion class by stilling and quieting the mind

- Familiarize students with their here-and-now stone in preparation for the exercise later in class

- Help students create community and connection

Instructions

- As students arrive to class, invite them to choose a here-and-now stone from your bag. Alternatively, you can pass out polished stones to students.

- Instruct students to carefully draw the stone, paying close attention to its lines, shadows, and so on.

- Emphasize that the intention is not the quality of the drawing—it is the act of mindfully paying attention—on purpose—and using their senses to notice what they are observing.

- Since this is a mindful art activity, it is important to periodically guide students to notice the physical sensations they experience while they are drawing. Ask questions such as:

  o Notice the feeling of the pencil in your hand. What does it feel like in the places where it touches your hand?

  o Perhaps notice the pressure of the pencil against the paper. Play around with using a stronger or lighter pressure. What do you notice?

  o How does it feel where you are gripping the pencil? Is there pressure there? Does it feel tense? If so, what does it feel like when you loosen your grip?

  o If your hand is feeling tense or uncomfortable, what does it feel like to stretch out your hand and give it a bit of a break?

  o What does the place where your hand is touching the paper or desk feel like? Does it feel cool or warm to the touch? Hard? Smooth?

Mindful Eating

5 minutes (practice)
5 minutes (discussion)

Intention

- Cultivate an awareness that our senses are a portal to the present moment

Instructions

- Read the following script to students:

Keeping in mind the lessons we've learned about mindfulness in the previous sessions, today we are going to explore a practice that engages the senses, because the senses are a way that we can experience the present moment.

In fact, we are going to pretend that we are aliens from another planet, and we have landed here on this little planet called Earth. As I walk around the room, open your hand, and lo and behold, you will find that a small item lands on it. You have no idea what this item is because you have never seen it before.

First, notice what you are feeling as I put a few of these items in your hand.

[Place a few dried cranberries, grapes, or a mandarin orange in each person's hand. As you go through the next series of questions, provide ample time between questions for students to respond.]

What does your sense of touch tell you about this object? Is it light, heavy, dense, small, or round? What does it feel like? What's the texture like? Is it the same texture all over, or is it different in places?

Now you are going to explore this object with your sense of sight. What do you see? What color is it? Is it the same color all over, or are there different shades? What happens when you hold it up to the light?

Now you will use your sense of smell. How would you describe its scent? If it's hard to detect a smell, maybe smell a few of them together. It will make the smell stronger. You're simply exploring this with curiosity. Remember, you're aliens and have just landed here.

Do you notice any salivation happening in your mouth, or is your mouth dry? Are you already noticing changes in your mouth as you simply smell this object?

Next, you are going to use your sense of hearing. Roll this object between your fingers, next to your ear. What do you hear? How would you describe this sound? Try both ears. Is it different from one ear to the other? Remember, you can't compare this to something here on Earth because you're an alien who is unfamiliar with everything on Earth.

Since we've been playing with this object for a bit, you may want to use a different one of these objects for the next step.

Now take this item and place it in your mouth. Let it just sit there for a moment. Notice the taste before you take a bite. How would you describe it? Notice what you're feeling and thinking. What's the texture in your mouth? Notice any sensations.

Now, take a bite. What happens? [If the fruit is fresh, they will likely get a burst of flavor.]

Slowly, turn this object over in your mouth, noticing its texture and taste. If you're okay with doing this silently with your eyes closed, it's often easier to get in touch with what you're actually sensing.

As you move the object around your mouth, notice when the urge to swallow begins. Keep noticing what's happening with the item as it eventually dissolves.

Discussion

- What did you notice as you were going through this process?

- What is it like to pay this much attention to something?

- How was this experience different from the way that you normally eat?

- What would it be like if you paid this much attention to other aspects of your life? For example, conversations with your family, schoolwork, sports?

Teaching Tip: Fresh, recently purchased fruit will work best for this practice, as it will have the most flavor. It is okay if students don't like the fruit you choose. The objective of the activity is not to have the teens "like" the food. The objective is for them to pay attention with all their senses. If the food is not appealing to them, this becomes something for them to note and observe.

Please do not use candy or chocolate, as this may elicit a strong emotional response. You want the object to be neutral so students can more easily observe their responses, rather than be distracted by "loving" or "hating" the object. You can also use raisins, but I have found that some students have strong aversions to raisins, which then becomes a distraction as well.

Finally, teens sometimes need clarification between the senses. For example, they may give an example of sense of touch when discussing sense of sight. Clarify with humor.

Compassionate Body Scan

10 minutes (practice)
5 minutes (inquiry)

Intention

- Bring mindful awareness to physical sensations in the body

Instructions

- Read the following script to students:

    Just like we observed the dried cranberries with our senses (and just like we noticed the sensations in the soles of our feet), we're now going to observe the sensations in other parts of our body. We do this because we have to first be aware of our direct experience before we can turn toward ourselves with kindness. Mindfulness is about being aware of an experience as it is happening.

    To begin, put your head on your desk with your arms folded under your head, or get into some other position that allows you to be in your own quiet and private space.

    Now, see if you can find the place on your body where you can notice your breath most easily. This might be at the tip of your nose as you're breathing in, or maybe it's inside your nostrils, or maybe it's in the slight rising and falling of your chest as your lungs expand and contract. Maybe it's the feeling of your belly rising and falling with each in-breath and each out-breath.

    If it feels comfortable for you, perhaps place a hand over your heart as a way of bringing a gentle, kind attitude toward yourself. Or if you'd prefer, put a fist over your heart, with your other hand on top of it, to remind yourself that self-compassion is about being strong and loving toward yourself.

    Now, take three deep, relaxing breaths. Then you can place your arm under your head again if that feels okay.

    Now, shift your attention from your belly all the way down through your legs, ankles, and feet, working to the soles of your feet. Notice any sensations that are here in the soles of your feet. Are they warm or cool? Dry or moist?

    Now, bring a measure of gratitude to your feet. Your feet have such a small surface area, yet they hold up your entire body all day long. Our feet work hard for us, although we rarely pay any attention to them. If your feet feel good today, you can also extend gratitude that you don't have discomfort.

    As you inhale, shift your attention from your feet up into your ankles, calves, and shins. First on one foot, and then the next.

Whenever you notice that your mind has wandered, as it will after a few moments, just return to the sensations in your legs.

If you notice yourself judging or not liking any particular part of your body, see if you can allow those feelings to simply be there without pushing them away. If that's too hard, it's totally fine to move on to another part of your body.

Now, returning to your legs, simply become aware of sensations of touch where your legs are in contact with the chair you're sitting in. What do those points of contact feel like? Is there pressure there? Maybe even a little pain? Maybe a feeling of coolness? Maybe warmth?

As you inhale, shift up to your knees, thighs, and hips, noticing what is here in the way of sensation.

Can you bring gratitude to your legs, hips, and feet for all the support they offer you in each moment? How they work to take you from place to place?

Shift now into your belly, becoming aware of your belly expanding and contracting as you breathe, nourishing you with each in-breath and soothing and relaxing you with each out-breath.

And, now, shift your attention to your chest, noticing your lungs expanding and contracting, and your heart beating. Can you simply feel this body just as it is, breathing and beating? Offer a moment of kindness to your lungs and heart for their strength and the effort they make, keeping you alive.

Think about it—this heart has been beating only for you! And it has been beating since before you were born and likely hasn't stopped the whole time you've been alive. Amazing, isn't it?

Now, shift your attention into your neck, throat, and head. Become aware of the neck that supports your head and the throat that allows you to talk, swallow, and breathe. Your eyes that see, your nose that breathes, your mouth that eats, your ears that hear, and your lips that speak.

Now that you have paid kind attention to each individual part, put your hand on your heart again and give your entire body a final shower of affection.

When you're ready, gently open your eyes.

- Break the students into small groups and discuss what the experience was like. Offer two to three minutes to discuss. Alternatively, keep students in a large group, and ask for volunteers to share their experience.

Inquiry

- What happened when you paid attention to each body part? What did you notice?

- Did your mind wander?

- What did you do when your mind wandered?

Wandering Mind

5 minutes

Intention

- Explain the first insight of mindfulness—that the mind wanders

Talking Points

- The wandering mind is often referred to as the "monkey mind" because it swings from one branch of thought to the next. Ask students to imagine what monkeys are like when they jump from treetop to treetop.

- The mind wanders when it is at rest, and generally it wanders into the past or the future.

- When it wanders to the future, it generally is worrying about something that might happen. Since the brain is hardwired for our survival, it is always scanning the environment for potential threats. It is looking for things that can hurt us so we can be prepared when they come up. But this also causes worry and anxiety. It can lead us to engage in catastrophic thinking, where we think obsessively about irrational or worst-case outcomes.

- When the mind wanders into the past, it thinks about things that we said or did that we think we shouldn't have—things that we regret. We repetitively go over this thought in our minds, which is a process called rumination. But rumination is strongly linked to depression. When people are depressed, they often have thoughts about being inadequate or worthless.

- So a wandering mind leads us to *worry* about things that might go wrong in the future or *ruminate* on things that have gone wrong in the past.

- By staying in the present moment, we're less likely to worry about something that might happen in the future or ruminate about something that happened in the past. As a result, we're less likely to experience anxiety or depression. To stay in the present moment, we simply notice the physical sensations we're having right here, right now. Physical sensations can only take place in the present moment.

- To help students keep their minds in the present moment rather than wandering to the past and future, let them know that they have a tool—a here-and-now stone, which they will explore in the next practice.

Teaching Tip: Depending on students' age and development, you can share the following findings from an article in *Science* magazine (Killingsworth & Gilbert, 2010). Researchers developed an iPhone app that contacted 2,250 volunteers at random intervals and asked what they were doing, if they were aware of what they were doing, and if they were happy. On average, researchers found that participants' minds wandered 46.9 percent of the time, and most of that time, they weren't happy.

Here-and-Now Stone

5 minutes

Intention

- Practice anchoring attention to a focal object as a way of staying in the present moment

Instructions

- Invite students to take out the stone that they chose as they arrived to class. Then read the following script to students:

Start by carefully examining your stone, noticing its colors, its angles, and the way the light plays on its curves. Let yourself really enjoy the beauty of the stone.

Now, closing your eyes if you're okay with that, explore the stone with your sense of touch. What does it feel like? Is it smooth or rough? What is its temperature?

Then, opening your eyes, let yourself become absorbed in your stone. Allow yourself to appreciate the age of your stone. Some may be almost as old as the Earth itself!

Notice that when you are focused on your stone in this way, there is no regret or worry in this moment. You aren't stressing. For this reason, they are called here-and-now stones. They bring you to the present moment when you aren't in your head worrying about the past or ruminating about the future. Remember that physical sensations bring you to the present moment!

- Let students know that they are free to take these stones with them after the practice. They can keep them in their backpack, in their jacket pocket, or next to their bed. Some students use them when they wake up in the middle of the night and can't sleep. Some teens have also shared that the stones are really great at reducing anxiety before tests.

> **Teaching Tip:** You can provide students with mini flashlights and darken the room as a way of adding a dramatic effect while students explore the stones. This practice can also be done with any small, simple object, such as a pencil, a pen, a piece of jewelry, or even the palm of the hand. For detailed instructions on using the palm of the hand, see the mindfulness practices in chapter 5.

2 minutes

Intention

- Reinforce skills learned in the session

Instructions

- Encourage students to practice 5 to 10 minutes of formal practice per day, in addition to practicing informally throughout the week. Explain that the formal practices support the informal practices. Encourage them to try out the new practices learned in this session, but also to practice those tools that work best for them. Ultimately, the goal is for students to try them all but to hold on to and use those that they are most comfortable with.

- New tools for the toolkit: *Mindful Eating; Compassionate Body Scan; Here-and-Now Stone*

Toolkit	
Informal Tools	**Formal Tools**
1. Supportive Gestures	1. Sunbathing
2. Good Friend Question (Ask yourself: How would I treat a friend?)	2. Compassionate Friend
3. Sound Practice	3. Compassionate Body Scan
4. Soles of the Feet	
5. Mindful Eating	
6. Here-and-Now Stone	

Wrap-Up

- What will you take away from this session? [*Ask for a volunteer to start, and then go around the room, with each student offering something that stands out to them about this session. Give students the option to pass if they do not want to share. If time is limited, ask just a few students to respond.*]

 **SESSION 5**

The Adolescent Brain

Session Overview

- *Opening Art Activity*: Mindful Brain Coloring (10 min)

- *Topic*: When Self-Compassion Can Be Difficult (5 min)

- *Topic*: The Developing Teen Brain (15 min)

- *Formal Practice*: Affectionate Breathing (10 min)

- *Informal Practice*: Three Soothing Breaths (3 min)

- *Home Practice* (2 min)

In This Session, You Will . . .

- Discuss the development of the adolescent brain and the unique challenges and circumstances associated with this developmental period

- Offer several more mindfulness practices

Materials

- Video clip from *The Croods* (2013)

- *Mindful Brain Coloring Sheet*

- Colored pencils

Mindful Brain Coloring

10 minutes

Intention

- Help teens transition from their regular class to self-compassion class by stilling and quieting the mind

Instructions

- Pass out the *Mindful Brain Coloring Sheet* on the next page and provide students with colored pencils.

- Encourage students to color the brain however they would like, reminding them to notice the lines, shading, and colors they choose.

- As this is a mindfulness activity, it is about *noticing* what they are doing as they are doing it.

Mindful Brain Coloring Sheet

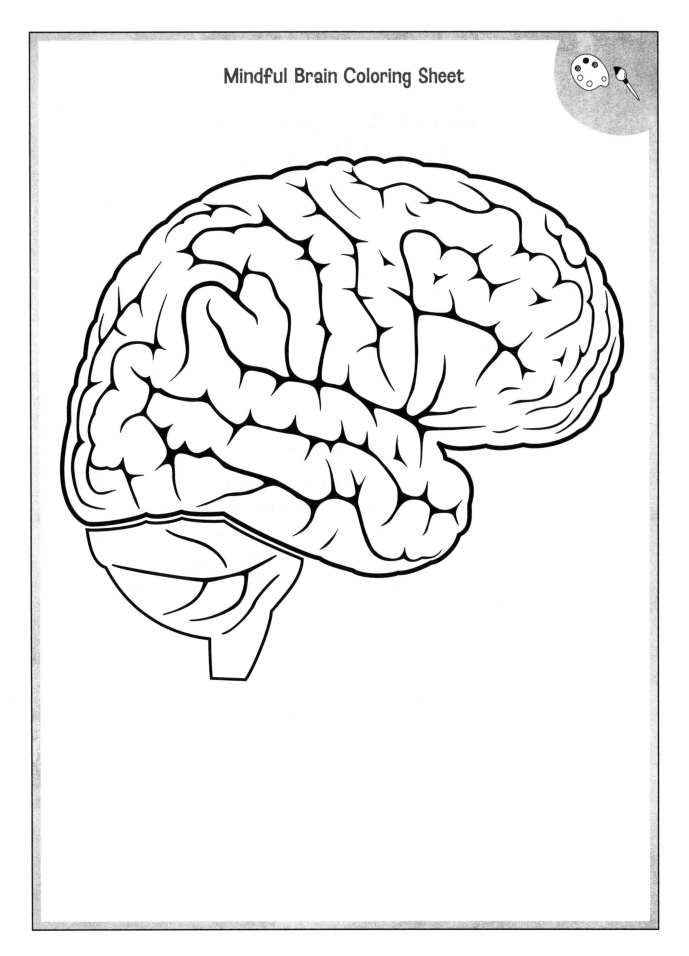

When Self-Compassion Can Be Difficult

5 minutes

Intention

- Help teens understand that strong and difficult emotions can arise suddenly when we begin to practice self-compassion

- Help teens understand that working with strong and difficult emotions is part of how we can begin to change how these emotions affect us

- Offer grounding practices to use when teens are experiencing strong emotions or difficult sensations

Talking Points

- When we begin to turn toward ourselves with kindness and compassion, we can begin to remember all the times when we *weren't* kind to ourselves. This can make us feel bad because it's like we are grieving for the ways we weren't so kind to ourselves before.

- If we have had feelings of self-doubt, or even self-hatred, when we offer ourselves kind words instead, it can open the door to our hearts, and some of the feelings we have been holding back can begin to come out.

- You can think of this as what you might do if a friend were to come over. Maybe you would quickly clean up our room and stuff all of the mess in your closet. Then what would happen the next time you opened the closet? Everything would come flying out.

- That means the difficult feelings that come out when practicing self-compassion are not caused by self-compassion—we're simply reexperiencing feelings that were already there and that we may have been hiding from.

- It can be very helpful to recognize this, especially when we are offering ourselves kindness, so that we can allow these feelings to surface and begin to heal. There is a slogan for this: "What we feel, we can heal, and what we resist can persist."

- So what can we do when we start feeling these difficult feelings?

    o   If the feelings are tolerable, we can allow them to just be there and keep practicing. We can notice the sadness, or the grief—whatever emotion is there. Simply notice it and give ourselves compassion for all the times in the past when we weren't supportive to ourselves.

    o   If the feelings feel too strong, we can practice mindfulness by noticing the soles of our feet or our here-and-now stones, for example. We can choose to focus our attention on something outside ourselves. Sometimes choosing an object on the other side of the room—farther away from us—is helpful.

    o   Alternatively, we can do "behavioral self-compassion," which means take a walk, listen to music, call a friend, or read a book. It's best to ask ourselves the fundamental self-compassion question ("What do I need right now?") and then act accordingly.

The Developing Teen Brain

15 minutes

Intention

- Help students understand that adolescent brain development is partly responsible for the emotional changes that they experience

- Explain to students that the adolescent brain is hardwired to get teenagers ready to leave home and take on adult responsibilities

Talking Points

Video Clip

- Play a video clip from the movie *The Croods* (2013), which can be accessed through various movie providers. Start at 9:08 (after "It's okay, I ate last week . . . ") and end at 13:30 ("Good man, Thunk").

- After watching the clip, ask students:

  ○ What stands out to you about this video clip?

  ○ How does the role of the father (i.e., to keep Eep safe) conflict with the role of Eep (i.e., to explore, try new things, and take risks)?

  ○ Does this video clip remind you of anything in your own life?

  ○ How can self-compassion help in these kinds of situations?

  ○ Does anyone know anything about what's going on in the brain during the teen years?

Adolescent Development

- During adolescence, the brain is very active and goes through many changes. Its primary purpose is to get you to a place where you are ready for the responsibilities of adulthood.

- This means that the brain is hardwired to prepare us to leave home, move away from our parents, and move toward a peer group who will help us navigate the challenges of this period of life.

- From an evolutionary standpoint, peers are important because this group is where we ultimately may choose to find a partner and continue the species.

- How we choose a peer group can be, in part, based on how we feel about ourselves. The need to belong, which is basic to who we are as human beings, can sometimes override the selection of a peer group who supports us in a healthy way.

- Self-compassion can support us when we are going through this difficult but essential transition in life. Self-compassion helps us to not be so hard on ourselves when we make a mistake or when things don't work out the way we want them to.

- How is this new knowledge about the developing adolescent brain useful in helping you communicate with your family?

- When you struggle with a caregiver or sibling, how can self-compassion help?

Teaching Tip: In the discussion, it may come up that some parents do not keep their children safe. Unfortunately, this is sometimes a reality of our society. If this comes up, it is important to acknowledge it and use it as an opportunity to practice self-compassion. If you suspect a student feels unsafe in their home, please follow state and local protocol.

Affectionate Breathing

5 minutes (practice)
5 minutes (inquiry)

Intention

- Teach students how to focus their attention to calm the mind

- Incorporate this mindful breathing technique with a sense of soothing and appreciation for what the breath provides for us

Instructions

- Read the following script to students:

One way that you can deal with difficult feelings that come up during the transition of adolescence is by using mindfulness and self-compassion skills. This next practice will teach you some of those skills. It can help ground you when anxiety, frustration, or stress is high.

To begin, please sit comfortably in your chair. Sit upright but not so much that your back is stiff, imagining there is a string that extends from the crown of your head up to the ceiling. Make sure your shoulders are relaxed and not hunched. This position will support you in being alert and aware. If you're comfortable closing your eyes, feel free to close them. If you'd rather have your eyes open, it's best to keep your gaze downward so you're not distracted by things around you.

Take a few slow, easy breaths, noticing the breath where it is most obvious to you. Maybe it's the tip of your nose where you're breathing in, the rising and lowering of your chest with each breath, or the area around your diaphragm below your rib cage. Wherever you notice it most easily.

Just feeling the breath, from the beginning of the in-breath all the way to the end of the out-breath.

Whenever your mind wanders, which it will because that's what minds do, gently bring your attention back to the breath.

Letting go of your need to control the breath in any way. Letting your body breathe itself, noticing how it naturally nourishes your body.

Feeling your whole body breathe, gently moving with the rising and falling of the breath, like the movement of the sea.

Noticing how the breath nourishes us and takes care of us and has been doing this our whole lives.

Letting yourself relax into the breath, as you would under a warm blanket.

And now, just release the breath, allowing everything that comes to awareness to be just as it is, just for now.

Slowly and gently open your eyes.

- As a large group, discuss what this practice was like.

Inquiry

- Were you able to feel your breath, even for a second?

- What was that like?

- Did your mind wander? What did you do when you noticed it was wandering?

Three Soothing Breaths

3 minutes

Intention

- To provide an informal variation of *Affectionate Breathing* that students can use in the moment when they feel stressed, upset, or anxious

Instructions

- This practice is an informal version of *Affectionate Breathing* that students can use any time they are beginning to feel upset, stressed, or anxious. Alternatively, they can use it as a grounding practice any time they just want to practice—it is available to use when needed.

- Read the following script to students to introduce them to the practice:

Begin by finding your breath where it is most apparent to you, whether that's the tip of your nose, your chest, or your diaphragm area.

Feel your breath from the very beginning of your in-breath to the very end of your out-breath, even noticing the places where your in-breath turns into your out-breath. And perhaps notice the place where your out-breath ends before the next in-breath begins.

What happens at the point where the in-breath turns into the out-breath?

See if you can pay attention to just one breath at first—one breath at a time. Then do this for the next breath, and then the next. Three breaths.

Teaching Tip: Often, teens prefer *Three Soothing Breaths* to *Affectionate Breathing*. If this is the case, it's fine for them to just practice the former. Using the breath as an anchor feels somewhat abstract for some students, so for this reason it is important to introduce less abstract practices earlier (e.g., *Here-and-Now Stone*, *Supportive Gestures*, *Compassionate Body Scan*). Developmentally, this makes sense, as abstract thinking doesn't develop until the second decade of life.

---

2 minutes

Intention

- Reinforce skills learned in the session

Instructions

- Encourage students to notice when they begin to feel anxious or upset and practice *Three Soothing Breaths*. (Even one soothing breath helps, but they can aim for three!)

- Ask students to try to practice 5 to 10 minutes of formal practice per day, in addition to practicing informally throughout the week.

- New tools for the toolkit: *Affectionate Breathing; Three Soothing Breaths*

Toolkit	
Informal Tools	**Formal Tools**
1. Supportive Gestures	1. Sunbathing
2. Good Friend Question (Ask yourself: How would I treat a friend?)	2. Compassionate Friend
3. Sound Practice	3. Compassionate Body Scan
4. Soles of the Feet	4. Affectionate Breathing
5. Mindful Eating	
6. Here-and-Now Stone	
7. Three Soothing Breaths	

Wrap-Up

- What will you take away from this session? [*Ask for a volunteer to start, and then go around the room, with each student offering something that stands out to them about this session. Give students the option to pass if they do not want to share. If time is limited, ask just a few students to respond.*]

 **SESSION 6**

Kindness

Session Overview

- *Opening Art Activity*: Kindness Phrases (10 min)
- *Formal Practice*: Kindness for Someone You Care About (15 min)
- *Topic*: Practicing with Kindness Phrases (5 min)
- *Informal Practice*: Finding Kindness Phrases (15 min)
- *Home Practice* (2 min)

In This Session, You Will . . .

- Help students find kindness phrases that work for them
- Reinforce the importance of extending kindness to oneself

Materials

- Calligraphy pens or thin markers
- White paper (make sure this will work with the calligraphy pens)
- *Kind Words List*

OPENING ART ACTIVITY

Kindness Phrases

10 minutes

Intention

- Help teens transition from their regular class to self-compassion class by stilling and quieting the mind

- Preview kindness words that will be used later in the session

Instructions

- Provide students with a list of kindness words or phrases, and invite them to choose a couple that resonate with them. There is a *Kind Words List* on the following page that you can photocopy to give to students.

- Provide students with inexpensive calligraphy pens (or alternatively thin markers, but calligraphy pens are more fun).

- Have them play with writing their chosen words on paper or in their notebooks. These words will be integrated into the kindness practice later in the session.

Kind Words List

Kindness	Self-compassion
Compassion	Happy
Ease of mind	Loved
Accepting myself	Belonging
Learning to accept myself	Confidence
Acceptance	Support
Safe	Connected
Courage	Fitting in
Peaceful	Brave
Strong	Healthy
Being myself	Calm
Comforted	Resilient
Centered	Joy
Serene	Authentic
Kind	At ease
Composed	

Kindness for Someone You Care About

10 minutes (practice)
5 minutes (inquiry)

Intention

- Help teens who have difficulty offering kindness to themselves

- Activate feelings of kindness by having students focus on an easy target (someone they care about) and then gently add themselves to the circle of kindness

Instructions

- Read the following script to students:

Get into a comfortable position sitting in your chair. If you'd like, you can put your head on your desk. Fully or partially close your eyes, taking a few deep breaths to settle into your body and into the present moment.

Now, bring to mind a being you care about or someone who naturally makes you smile. Someone with whom you have a comfortable and easy relationship—not necessarily a "perfect" relationship, because of course there's no such thing—but someone who just brings a lightness to your heart when you think of them.

This could be a child you know, a grandparent, your cat or dog—whoever naturally brings happiness to your heart. It doesn't have to be someone you know well. It could simply be someone in one of your classes who makes you laugh. If you have multiple persons you can't decide between, just choose one for now. You can always do this practice later with someone else.

I invite you to create a vivid image of this being in your mind, letting yourself feel what it's like to be in this being's presence. Allow yourself to enjoy the good company.

Now recognize how this being wishes to be happy and free from struggles, just like you and every other living being. Then repeat these wishes silently to yourself, for the other being, feeling the importance of your words: "I wish for you to be happy. I wish for you to feel loved. I wish for you to feel okay, just as you are." [Repeat twice, slowly.]

Whenever you notice that your mind has wandered, return to the words and the image of someone you care about, savoring any warm feelings that may arise and taking your time.

Now add yourself to your circle of good wishes. Create an image of yourself in the presence of the being you care about, visualizing both of you together. Extend the same goodwill to both of you: "I wish for us to be happy. I wish for us to feel loved. I wish for us to feel okay, just as we are." [Repeat twice, slowly.]

Now, letting go of the image of the other being, allow the full focus of your attention to rest directly on yourself. Put your hand over your heart, feeling the warmth and gentle pressure of your hand. Visualize your whole body in your mind's eye, noticing any stress or uneasiness that may be lingering within you, and offer yourself the phrases: "I wish to be happy. I wish to feel loved. I wish to feel okay, just as I am." [Repeat twice, slowly.]

Finally, taking a few breaths and just resting quietly in your own body, accept whatever your experience is, exactly as it is. You may be feeling good wishes and compassion, or you may not—it doesn't matter. We are simply setting an intention to open our hearts and see what happens.

When you're ready, gently open your eyes if they've been closed.

Inquiry

- What was it like to wish good things for someone else?

- What was it like to wish good things for both someone else and yourself?

- How about when you were just wishing good things for yourself? What was that like?

- Did anyone have difficulty feeling kindness with this practice?

- If the kindness phrases we used don't work for you, no worries! You'll have the chance to find phrases that speak to you in the next exercise.

Teaching Tip: (*optional*) You can explain to students a Jewish story that illustrates how the practice works: A disciple asks the rabbi, "Why does the Torah tell us to 'place these words upon your hearts?' Why does it not tell us to place these holy words *in* our hearts?" The rabbi answers, "It is because as we are, our hearts are closed, and we cannot place the holy words in our hearts. So we place them on top of our hearts. And there they stay until, one day, the heart breaks and the words fall in."

Practicing with Kindness Phrases

5 minutes

Intention

- Establish guidelines for discovering personal kindness phrases
- Provide the foundation for the exercise that follows

Talking Points

- Just as we can use the breath to anchor our attention to the present moment, we can use kindness phrases to anchor our attention to the present moment as well.

- The phrases should be clear, simple, honest, and kind. We don't want to say something that might create an argument in our minds when we practice kindness.

- We can think of kindness phrases as intentions of goodwill that we extend toward ourselves: "I wish for this to be so." As the mindfulness teacher Sharon Salzberg says, it's like giving yourself a birthday card that says, "Here, I'm wishing you well!"

- Kindness phrases are a bit different from positive affirmations, which state something that we want. We have to be careful not to set up an argument in our minds by stating something that we don't believe to be true or pretending things are different from the way they are.

- For example, if we say, "I am strong," but we don't believe this to be true, a little voice will creep up inside us and say, "Who are you kidding? You're not strong!" That's a clue that the phrase needs to be changed or modified so that it is a wish, rather than an affirmation, so there isn't an argument in our minds. Examples of modifications could be:

  - I wish to be strong.
  - I wish to one day be strong.
  - I wish to begin to feel strong.
  - I wish to one day begin to believe that I can be strong.

- The phrases should also be more general than specific. For example, "I wish to be happy" (general) versus "I wish to be free of anxiety or depression" (specific).

- Finally, any phrases that involve accepting ourselves, like "I wish to begin to accept myself, just as I am," refer to who we are as the most basic, deepest form of ourselves—not about any *behaviors* we have.

- We want to say these expressions slowly and warmly toward ourselves, perhaps the way we would to a dear friend who needed some support.

- Remember that we are simply setting an intention, a wish for ourselves. That's all.

- In the next practice, we will find kindness phrases that work for us.

Teaching Tip: Students may just want to say one word of kindness to themselves, rather than phrases.

Finding Kindness Phrases

10 minutes (practice)
5 minutes (discussion)

Intention

- Discover short kindness phrases that are deeply meaningful—ones that students would genuinely want and need to hear over and over again

Instructions

- Read the following script to students:

To begin, close your eyes if you're okay with that and, if it is comfortable and feels right for you, place your hand on your heart or use a different comforting gesture—one that is comfortable for you right now.

Settling on your breath for a few moments, feel the breath moving into your chest and perhaps bring an awareness to your hand over your heart. Notice how this hand, heart, and breath move together.

Now, ask yourself, "What is it that I would I like to hear right now? What words would make me feel most comforted and supported?" Or maybe another way of asking this would be "What words would I like to hear every day for the rest of my life if I could?"

When you feel ready, please open your eyes if they were closed and write down a word or phrase that may have come to mind for you.

You may want to use one of the words you wrote down in the art activity at the beginning of the session.

Now, see if you can create a wish for yourself from the words that came to you. For example, if the words that you want to hear are "I'm a good person," this can become "I wish to know deep in myself that I am a good person."

These wishes are for you only, no one else. Make them your own and see if you can offer yourself kindness, support, or warmth that would feel like putting on a warm jacket when you're cold—something that is soothing and supportive when you need to be soothed and supported. For example:

- ○ *"I wish to know that I am safe."*
- ○ *"I wish to know I can accept myself, just as I am."*
- ○ *"I wish to know that I am worthy and lovable."*

If it is difficult to find words or a phrase that feel real to you, then introduce the possibility:

- ○ *"I wish to know I'm a good person" can become "I wish to begin to know what a good person I am."*

- ○ *"I wish to feel strong" can become "I wish to begin to know my own inner strength."*

- ○ *"I wish to know I'm lovable" can become "I wish to begin to love myself, just as I am."*

Remember that we are just beginning the journey of kindness toward ourselves and we want this to be easy, not difficult or challenging.

Now, write down any words or phrases that felt important for you to hear.

Remember the common humanity aspect of self-compassion. Everyone here has words they would like to or need to hear—maybe for the rest of their lives.

Discussion

- Were you able to find new kindness phrases?

- How do they make you feel when you hear them?

- If you weren't able to find kindness phrases this time, can you be okay with that, knowing that this is a process that might take some time?

HOME PRACTICE

2 minutes

Intention

- Reinforce skills learned in this session

Instructions

- Encourage students to practice 5 to 10 minutes of formal practice per day, in addition to practicing informally throughout the week.

- Suggest that students continue to explore the questions "What do I need to hear? What words would make me feel safe, comforted, and supported?" throughout the week. Finding kindness phrases is a process that takes some time. When students discover the right word or phrases, they will often want to respond with "Yes! That's just what I need to hear! Thank you!"

- New tools for the toolkit: *Kindness for Someone You Care About; Finding Kindness Phrases*

Toolkit	
Informal Tools	**Formal Tools**
1. Supportive Gestures	1. Sunbathing
2. Good Friend Question (Ask yourself: How would I treat a friend?)	2. Compassionate Friend
3. Sound Practice	3. Compassionate Body Scan
4. Soles of the Feet	4. Affectionate Breathing
5. Mindful Eating	5. Kindness for Someone You Care About
6. Here-and-Now Stone	
7. Three Soothing Breaths	
8. Finding Kindness Phrases	

Wrap-Up

- What will you take away from this session? [*Ask for a volunteer to start, and then go around the room, with each student offering something that stands out to them about this session. Give students the option to pass if they do not want to share. If time is limited, ask just a few students to respond.*]

 **SESSION 7**

Laying the Foundation for Self-Compassion

Session Overview

- *Opening Art Activity*: First Initial (10 min)
- *Formal Practice*: A Person Just Like Me (10 min)
- *Practice Discussion* (10 min)
- *Formal Practice*: Calming Music (10 min)
- *Home Practice* (2 min)

In This Session, You Will . . .

- Reinforce the concepts of mindfulness and kindness to establish a solid foundation for the next session
- Demonstrate the concept of common humanity

Materials

- Colored pencils and markers
- Black pens
- Instrumental music (e.g., "Silk Road" by Kitarō)
- Copy of the first letter of each student's name (*optional*)

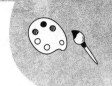

First Initial

10 minutes

Intention

- Help students transition from their regular class to self-compassion class by stilling and quieting the mind

- Cultivate mindfulness skills

Instructions

- Provide each student with an outline of the first letter of their first name. (Alternatively, they can draw their own first initial, but many students feel "seen" when they are given an outline of the first letter of their name.)

- Drawing mindfully, the students can then use a black pen or pencil to create designs within the letter and outside the letter. They should be drawing slowly and carefully, noticing the lines as they draw, the pressure of their hand on the pen or pencil, and the pressure of the pen or pencil against the paper. Throughout this activity, it's helpful to provide periodic reminders to notice these physical sensations.

- You may also ask students to notice any thoughts arising in their minds, such as "I wish I had done this differently," or "The design of the person next to me is so much nicer than mine." If they notice thoughts arising, encourage them to simply acknowledge that these are thoughts, not facts, and return their attention to their drawing.

- Students can add color with colored pencils or markers once the letter has been filled in with designs, but the objective is not to rush to "complete" the artwork—it is to draw slowly, carefully, and mindfully. Color can always be added at a later time.

- Emphasize that the intention is not about the quality of the artwork—it is the act of paying attention and transitioning to a more contemplative space and to prepare them for the class.

- The first five minutes of the activity can be chatty so students can socialize a bit, but the last few minutes should be silent so that students can more easily notice sensations.

A Person Just Like Me*

5 minutes (practice)
5 minutes (inquiry)

Intention

- Demonstrate common humanity

- Demonstrate compassion for others

Instructions

- Read the following script to students:

  Get into a comfortable seated position, then look around the room and silently select one person in the room to focus on for this practice.

  Now take a few deep breaths to relax.

  Close your eyes if that's okay with you, then bring to mind an image of this person.

  As you imagine this person, let's consider a few things about them:

    ○ *This person is a human being, just like me.*

    ○ *This person has a body and a mind, just like me.*

    ○ *This person has feelings, emotions, and thoughts, just like me.*

    ○ *This person has, at some point, been sad, disappointed, angry, hurt, or confused, just like me.*

    ○ *This person wishes to be free from pain and unhappiness, just like me.*

    ○ *This person wishes to be safe, healthy, and loved, just like me.*

    ○ *This person wishes to be happy, just like me.*

  Now, let's allow some wishes for this person to arise:

    ○ *I wish for this person to have the strength, resources, and support to help them through the difficult times in life.*

    ○ *I wish for this person to be free from pain and suffering.*

    ○ *I wish for this person to be strong and balanced.*

    ○ *I wish for this person to be happy because this person is a fellow human being, just like me.*

---

* From *Search Inside Yourself* by Chade-Meng Tan. Copyright © 2012 by Chade-Meng Tan. Used by permission of HarperCollins Publishers.

Take a few more deep breaths and notice what you're feeling.

Gently open your eyes if they've been closed.

Inquiry

- What was it like to notice that others in this room experience the same feelings as you?

- What do you think it would be like if you did this practice in your classroom every day for a different person? How do you think this might change things?

PRACTICE DISCUSSION

10 minutes

Intention

- Check in with students to see how their practice is progressing
- Offer possibilities of how they can meet their struggles with self-compassion

Instructions

- Invite participants to share their experiences of the two new home practices during the past week—*Finding Kindness Phrases* and *Kindness for Someone You Care About*—and to describe how their mindfulness and self-compassion practice is going in general.

- Specifically, ask:

  o Did anyone experience any stress this past week? Did you have moments where you felt even a little badly about yourself? Did you remember to use the kindness phrases? If so, how did that go?

  o Did you use any other practices that we've learned? Remember, we are filling our toolbox with an array of different practices—all for us to try out and see which ones we like. Some will likely work for us, and others may not. That's okay. Pick and choose the ones that work, and don't worry about the ones that don't. They may work at another time, or they may not. Different tools work for different people, in different situations.

  o Did you come up with any kindness phrases that work for you? If not, no worries! Sometimes finding the right words takes time. Keep asking yourself the question "What words do I need to hear to feel comforted and supported?"

Calming Music

5 minutes (practice)
5 minutes (inquiry)

Intention

- Allow students to comfort themselves while mindfully listening to music

Instructions

- Invite teens to find a comfortable seat, or if there's room on the floor, they can lie on their backs on a towel or yoga mat.

- Tell students that the instructions for this practice are to pay attention to the tones and sounds of the music, noticing the individual instruments in the piece. Whenever their mind wanders, encourage them to simply, without any judgment, return their attention back to the music.

- Begin to play a piece of instrumental music. The music should be soothing and melodic (for example, "Silk Road" by Kitarō).

- Remind students once or twice as the music plays to bring their attention back to listening to the sounds of the music.

Inquiry

- What was this like for you?

- How does your body feel after the practice?

- Did you notice your mind wandering? Were you able to bring it back?

- Did you observe any self-judgment when you noticed your mind wandering?

- Did you notice any reactions to the music—pleasant or unpleasant? How did you know?

- How do you think you can incorporate this practice into your life?

Teaching Tip: Since music is very personal, encourage students to create a playlist of music that they find relaxing and soothing. The only caveat is that it needs to be instrumental. Words take us into our heads, and you want students to focus attention to their bodies, where they can access their senses.

2 minutes

Intention

- Reinforce skills learned in this session

Instructions

- Encourage students to practice 5 to 10 minutes of formal practice per day, in addition to practicing informally throughout the week.

- Encourage students to create a playlist of calming instrumental music pieces they can listen to for music meditation.

- To continue growing the common humanity component of self-compassion, encourage students to try out *A Person Just Like Me* with different people over the course of the next week.

- New tools for the toolkit: *A Person Just Like Me; Calming Music*

Toolkit	
Informal Tools	**Formal Tools**
1. Supportive Gestures	1. Sunbathing
2. Good Friend Question (Ask yourself: How would I treat a friend?)	2. Compassionate Friend
3. Sound Practice	3. Compassionate Body Scan
4. Soles of the Feet	4. Affectionate Breathing
5. Mindful Eating	5. Kindness for Someone You Care About
6. Here-and-Now Stone	6. A Person Just Like Me
7. Three Soothing Breaths	7. Calming Music
8. Finding Kindness Phrases	

Wrap-Up

- What will you take away from this session? [*Ask for a volunteer to start, and then go around the room, with each student offering something that stands out to them about this session. Give students the option to pass if they do not want to share. If time is limited, ask just a few students to respond.*]

 **SESSION 8**

Self-Compassion

Session Overview

- *Opening Art Activity*: Drawing to Music (10 min)

- *Topic*: Self-Compassion (5 min)

- *Topic*: Self-Criticism and Safety (5 min)

- *Exercise*: Motivating Ourselves with Compassion (20 min)

- *Home Practice* (2 min)

In This Session, You Will . . .

- Demonstrate how self-compassion can work in modifying behavior

Materials

- Paper

- Pencils, colored pencils, and crayons

- Instrumental music (e.g., "Silk Road" by Kitarō)

Drawing to Music

10 minutes

Intention

- Help students transition from their regular class to self-compassion class by stilling and quieting the mind

- Cultivate mindfulness skills

Instructions

- Play an instrumental piece of music, such as "Silk Road" by Kitarō or another piece of relaxing, instrumental music.

- Instruct students to listen closely to the music as they draw, allowing themselves to "feel" the music in their bodies and allowing the feeling to influence how they draw.

- They can use regular pencils, colored pencils, or crayons. (Markers are not recommended as they do not provide for gradation or variability.)

- Periodically remind students that when their minds wander, they should return their attention to hearing the tones of the music, the different instruments in the piece, and the different melody or harmony lines.

Self-Compassion

5 minutes

Intention

- Review the definition of self-compassion and the three components of self-compassion

Talking Points

- Self-compassion involves treating ourselves as we would treat a good friend who is struggling.

- Self-compassion is *not* about burying or pushing away bad feelings, as tempting as this might be. Rather, it's about allowing ourselves to be with these uncomfortable feelings, even for a little bit, and to offer ourselves the care and support we need as we feel these feelings.

- This is an important distinction—we do not offer ourselves compassion to make the suffering go away. We offer ourselves compassion simply *because* we are suffering, just as a good parent would be present and caring with a sick child.

- Self-compassion is both tender and strong at the same time. It's self-compassionate to stand up for ourselves if we're in a toxic friendship, for example. It's even self-compassionate to decide not to be friends with that person anymore if we feel that the friendship is hurting us.

- Remember that the three components of self-compassion are:
  - Self-kindness (vs. self-criticism)
  - Common humanity (vs. isolation)
  - Mindfulness (vs. overidentification)

- People often have doubts about self-compassion because we have not been raised to be kind to ourselves. Rather, we have been raised to be kind to others. It's important to address these doubts by talking about what self-compassion is not.

- Self-Compassion is *not*:

  ○ A motivation killer! We will not become couch potatoes if we're more self-compassionate. In fact, research has shown the opposite. Teens who are more self-compassionate are *more* motivated to work hard and try new things. This is likely because they know that if they fail, they're not going to beat themselves up. They can acknowledge that this particular challenge did not work out, and they can then move on.

  ○ Self-pity. When people get caught in self-pity, they feel sorry for themselves and forget that other people in the world go through similar difficulties. In contrast, self-compassion says, "Yes, your life may be hard right now, but you are not alone. Part of life involves struggle, and we all struggle at times. It's not you. It's life."

  ○ Selfish or self-serving. When we practice self-compassion, we are actually able to be more giving because we feel stronger, steadier, and more centered—therefore increasing our capacity to reach out to others.

  ○ Self-indulgent. People who are more self-compassionate take better care of themselves. They eat healthier, go to doctors when they should, and maintain exercise routines. In other words, they treat themselves better!

Self-Criticism and Safety

5 minutes

Intention

- Help students explore and understand self-criticism as safety behavior

Talking Points

- We all have many parts to ourselves, each with their own voices. For example, we each have a critical part and a compassionate part.

- Today, we'll learn more about our critical or judgmental part (known as the *inner critic*) and also discover the loving and compassionate part of ourselves (known as the *compassionate voice*). We'll learn how we can begin to quiet our critic and cultivate compassion for ourselves.

- Do you think there is some value in self-criticism? If so, what is it? How might the inner critic serve you in some way? [*Emphasize that the inner critic is trying to keep us safe and protect us, even if it's not all that effective. Make sure the reasons below are brought out in the discussion.*]

  - It motivates us to improve.

  - It helps us behave better and avoid further criticism.

  - It provides an illusion of control: "If I had just tried harder, I would have been perfect."

  - It lowers expectations so we're less likely to disappoint ourselves.

  - It makes other people feel better so they like us more.

- In the next exercise, we'll have an opportunity to learn how to:

  - Deal more productively with the inner critic.

  - Motivate changes we'd like to make in ourselves from a place of care and compassion rather than harsh self-judgment and criticism.

EXERCISE

Motivating Ourselves with Compassion

15 minutes (exercise)
5 minutes (discussion)

Intention

- Understand the purpose of the inner critic part in order to meet it with compassion and work with it more effectively

- Cultivate a compassionate voice so students can offer themselves support and care when the inner critic arises

- Motivate and empower students to make adaptive changes from a place of care, kindness, and goodwill rather than judgment, harsh criticism, or shame

- Experience the dual aspects of self-compassion and how they work together

Instructions

- Read the following script to students:

Often, recalling the words of our inner critic naturally creates some discomfort. It's hard to replay the harsh words we say to ourselves. Throughout this exercise, remember to notice how you are feeling and to be kind to yourself. You may offer yourself the support of a comforting gesture, like a hand on the heart or abdomen. You may also support yourself with a kind word or phrase, like "I'm here for you" or "Safe"—whatever you most need to hear in the moment.

If you begin to feel too uncomfortable, you might choose to take a break from the exercise entirely and use Three Soothing Breaths *or* Soles of the Feet, *or focus on an object with all your senses, as we did with the* Here-and-Now Stone. *Or if you'd rather, you can think about what you're having for lunch! As always, please remember to take care of yourself—that's what self-compassion is about.*

To begin, make sure you have a pen and paper nearby. Then think about a behavior you would like to change, something you continue to beat yourself up about. It's important that you identify a behavior and not a characteristic you can't change, like having big feet. I won't be asking you to share this behavior with others, so please try to be honest with yourself.

Choose a behavior that you think is unhelpful, like:

  ○ *Procrastinating with schoolwork*

- *Spending too much time on social media*
- *Staying up too late at night*
- *Biting your fingernails*
- *Playing on your phone or with other things during class*
- *Forgetting to complete chores around the house (e.g., dishes, trash)*
- *Becoming irritable with people in your life*
- *Eating too much junk food*
- *Isolating yourself from people who care about you*

Your Inner Critic

Now please write down the words that the inner critic part of you typically says when you find yourself engaging in this behavior. How does it express itself? What tone does it use?

When you're done, take a moment to consider how much suffering that inner critic part has caused you so far.

Then try giving yourself compassion for how hard it is to continually hear such harsh criticism. You may choose to write some words of compassion and support, or you may repeat the words silently to yourself. For example, you might say something like:

- *This is so hard to deal with. I'm so sorry!*
- *You are dealing with so much right now.*
- *It's so hard to feel like you are at war with yourself and constantly beating yourself up.*
- *I don't want you to struggle anymore!*

If you're having a hard time with this and you have a pet, think of what your pet might say to comfort you. Pets often sense our discomfort and support us. So imagine what they might say if they could talk. Maybe something like "I care about you and I'm here to protect and comfort you." Or consider what a compassionate friend might say to you.

Take time to silently repeat these supportive words to yourself using a kind tone of voice, as you would with a good friend. You may also want to offer yourself a supportive gesture to feel some comfort.

Now consider for a moment that your inner critic part's intention in saying these harsh words might be to help you change this unhelpful behavior. Even if your inner critic part ultimately ends up hurting you, is it possible that it is trying to protect you or keep you safe in some way? Are there other ways your inner critic part might be trying to help you, even if the way it goes about doing so creates additional shame or distress for you?

If so, please write down how your inner critic part might be trying to keep you safe from some perceived risk or danger.

Sometimes the inner critic part's criticism seems to have no value whatsoever, so if you can't identify any way that it is trying to help you, please continue to give yourself compassion for how its criticism has caused you pain.

If you have identified some way your inner critic part might be trying to keep you safe or help you, see if you can acknowledge its effort and write down a few words of thanks. Let the inner critic part know that even though it may not be serving you very well now, you see that its intention is good and it is trying its best.

Your Compassionate Voice

Now that you've heard from one part of you, your inner critic part, what is the counter to that voice? A kinder voice? A part of you that's wise? A part that maybe recognizes that this behavior is causing you harm or getting in your way? A part that also wants you to change, but motivates you without shame or harsh criticism?

Close your eyes, if that feels comfortable to you, and offer yourself a supportive gesture. You might choose a gesture of strength by placing a fist over your heart or solar plexus, or you might choose a comforting gesture by placing a hand over your heart or holding your hands together. Choose whatever feels right to you in this moment.

What words might this wise, kind, and supportive voice use to encourage you to make a change? For example, "I really care about you and don't want you to struggle so much." Or maybe some fiercer words would be helpful, like "You deserve to know your own strength, and you have the right to be healthy. You can do what's best for you!"

What words of encouragement, empowerment, motivation, or strength do you need to hear?

If you're having a hard time with this, think about a favorite teacher, coach, or mentor who cares about you and wants the best for you. What would they say to encourage and support you in making this change? You might also consider someone you haven't met who inspires you and whom you respect. This might be a famous person, someone from history, or a character from a book or movie. What do you think they would say? Or you might think of what you'd say to motivate a good friend who wants to make the same change.

Take time to silently repeat these words to yourself. When you're ready, gently open your eyes if they've been closed.

Compassionate Letter Writing

Now, express your experience in writing. Begin to write freely and spontaneously in the voice of this compassionate part of yourself.

This exercise might feel a bit awkward at first because we are not so familiar speaking to ourselves from this kinder, more compassionate voice, but see if you can just allow yourself to write whatever words come to mind. It gets easier with practice.

If you've found some new words for your inner compassionate voice, let yourself savor the feeling of being supported.

If you are having trouble finding the words, that's okay too. It takes some time. In fact, it's good to take this in slowly. The important thing is that you set an intention to try to be kinder to yourself.

Discussion

- What was your experience of this exercise?

- Were you able to hear your inner critic part?

- Were you able to hear your compassionate voice? If so, was it helpful?

- What felt more "right" to you to use in this exercise—the tender aspect of self-compassion (comforting, soothing, validating) or the fiercer, stronger part (motivating, protecting, providing)?

Teacher Tip: If working with a large group, divide students into groups of three before starting the discussion. Let students know they don't have to share the behavior they desire to change or even the words that they said to themselves. Rather, they can simply share what the process of this exercise was like. This is also time to listen compassionately, so it is important to refrain from giving advice, such as suggesting to someone else what they might do to address the issue that they're struggling with.

---

2 minutes

Intention

• Reinforce skills learned in this session

Instructions

• Encourage students to practice 5 to 10 minutes of formal practice per day, in addition to practicing informally throughout the week.

• Ask students to practice compassionate letter writing:

  ○ A letter to themselves from themselves, as they did at the end of *Motivating Ourselves with Compassion* in class ("me to me").

  ○ A letter from a compassionate other to themselves. Encourage them to think of an imaginary friend who is unconditionally wise, loving, and compassionate, and write a letter to themselves from the perspective of this friend ("you to me").

  ○ A letter from their compassionate self to another. Encourage them to write a letter as if they were talking to a good friend struggling with the same concerns ("me to you").

• New tool for the toolkit: *Compassionate Letter Writing*

Toolkit	
Informal Tools	**Formal Tools**
1. Supportive Gestures	1. Sunbathing
2. Good Friend Question (Ask yourself: How would I treat a friend?)	2. Compassionate Friend
3. Sound Practice	3. Compassionate Body Scan
4. Soles of the Feet	4. Affectionate Breathing
5. Mindful Eating	5. Kindness for Someone You Care About
6. Here-and-Now Stone	6. A Person Just Like Me
7. Three Soothing Breaths	7. Calming Music
8. Finding Kindness Phrases	8. Compassionate Letter Writing

Wrap-Up

- What will you take away from this session? (Ask for a volunteer to start, and then go around the room, with each student offering something that stands out to them about this session. Give students the option to pass if they do not want to share. If time is limited, ask just a few students to respond.)

 **SESSION 9**

Self-Compassion vs. Self-Esteem

Session Overview

- *Opening Art Activity*: Mindful Drawing to Music (10 min)

- *Topic*: Self-Esteem vs. Self-Compassion (10 min)

- *Exercise*: The Cost of Social Comparison (15 min)

- *Exercise*: Social Media Exploration (10 min)

- *Home Practice* (2 min)

In This Session, You Will . . .

- Demonstrate the difference between self-esteem and self-compassion

- Explore the costs of comparing ourselves to others

Materials

- Pencils and paper

- Instrumental music (e.g., "Autumn" by George Winston)

- YouTube videos:

  ○ "Duke University Professor Explains 'Self-Compassion'" (https://www.youtube.com/watch?v=tAifaBhh2xo)

  ○ "Dove Evolution" (https://www.youtube.com/watch?v=iYhCn0jf46U)

  ○ "Try" by Colbie Caillat (https://www.youtube.com/watch?v=GXoZLPSw8U8)

  ○ "It's Alright" by Mother, Mother (https://www.youtube.com/watch?v=G5-KJgVsoUM)

Mindful Drawing to Music

10 minutes

Intention

- Help students transition from their regular class to self-compassion class by stilling and quieting the mind

- Cultivate mindfulness skills

Instructions

- Play a piece of instrumental music that has varying degrees of tempo and volume, such as "Autumn" by George Winston.

- When the music gets louder or feels stronger (or faster), instruct students to use a pencil and, with heavy pressure, draw freeform designs on the page. Ask them to notice how their hand feels as they hold the pencil and what they see as they draw on the page.

- When the music feels light (softer or slower, for example), have them use a light pressure to draw.

- Do this for several minutes.

- Then ask them to do the opposite—when the music feels heavy, loud, or fast (your choice), have them use a light pressure. When it gets light or soft or slow, have them use a heavy pressure.

- Ask students how it felt when they allowed the music to guide the pressure they used on the page versus when they did the opposite.

TOPIC

Self-Esteem vs. Self-Compassion

10 minutes

Intention

- Understand how comparing ourselves to others creates suffering

- Explore similarities and differences between self-compassion and self-esteem

Talking Points

- It has been said, "Comparison is the thief of joy." What this means is that when we compare ourselves with others, we feel dissatisfied with our own lives. When we feel someone has outperformed us—maybe they're better looking, in better shape, or better dressed—we feel "less than" and our self-esteem plummets.

- On the flip side, when we feel that we've outperformed someone else, we feel better than them, and our self-esteem improves.

- Therefore, self-esteem is dependent on performance. Generally, we only feel good about ourselves when we perform better than average. And we expect ourselves to perform better than average on everything. But this is impossible. We all can't perform better than average on everything, because then average wouldn't be average!

- It's also impossible to perform above average all the time because, as humans, there are times we will inevitably fail.

- That's why it is a problem to use self-esteem as a way to guide our sense of self and how we relate to ourselves.

- Another problem with basing our sense of self on social comparisons is that it also creates a sense of separation from others, a disconnect, at a time in life when we *especially* need connection and a sense of belonging. As humans, what we need more than anything is to feel connected with others. The need for connection is in our biology, our DNA.

- That is where self-compassion comes in. Unlike self-esteem, self-compassion doesn't involve comparing ourselves with others and doesn't lead us to feel isolated. When we are self-compassionate, we are kind to ourselves no matter what. We are there for ourselves regardless of how we perform. We're there for ourselves when we succeed or when we fail, and especially when we fail.

- [*Have teens watch the following video, in which Dr. Mark Leary, a retired psychology professor and self-compassion researcher at Duke University, talks about the difference between self-compassion and self-esteem: "Duke University Professor Explains 'Self-Compassion'" (https://www.youtube.com/watch?v=tAifaBhh2xo).*]

The Cost of Social Comparison

10 minutes (exercise)
5 minutes (discussion)

Intention

- Notice that distress arises when we compare ourselves with others

- Practice supporting ourselves when feeling distressed

Instructions

- Provide a brief summary of the talking points covered in the previous topic, then read the following script to students:

Now, let's explore how we treat ourselves when we feel that we don't measure up.

Close your eyes if that's comfortable for you, and notice your experience in your body, including any feelings or sensations that might be present. Notice the feelings of your arms touching the chair, your feet on the floor, or any other sensations that might be here for you in this moment.

Bring to mind a time when you felt like you did not measure up because you were comparing yourself with another. Get a good image in your mind of who was there and what was said, and notice any feelings or sensations in your body.

As you recall this incident, notice how you're feeling right now. Notice the sensations that arise in your body. Do you feel any tightness anywhere? Maybe a tightness in your throat or a heaviness in your stomach? What feelings do you notice? Anger? Hurt? Loneliness? Sadness?

Now, offer yourself a kind and supportive gesture, such as a hand over your heart, or whatever feels kind to you. Feel the warmth of your hand.

Simply ask yourself, "What words do I most need to hear right now? What words would make me feel comforted or supported?" And if you can't think of the right words, maybe think of what you might say to a good friend struggling with something similar. Or maybe if you have a pet, think of what your pet might say to you if they saw that you were struggling. Now can you say those words to yourself?

Offer yourself these kind words just because you're feeling bad, just because you're struggling. And if saying these words feels strange or uncomfortable, say them anyway, and see what happens.

When you're done, gently open your eyes.

Remember that you can do this anytime you are feeling inadequate, not enough, or like you don't measure up. Simply ask yourself what you most need to hear right now, or what a friend or pet would say to you, and say those words to yourself.

- After this practice, show "Dove Evolution" (https://www.youtube.com /watch?v=iYhCn0jf46U). This video is intended to reinforce the point that we cannot possibly meet the many expectations that we have for ourselves because they are often unrealistic:

- As time allows, show one or both of the following YouTube videos:

    o "Try" by Colbie Caillat (https://www.youtube.com/watch?v=GXoZLPSw8U8)

    o "It's Alright" by Mother, Mother (https://www.youtube.com/watch?v=G5 -KJgVsoUM)

Discussion

- What if you could feel good about yourself *without* comparing yourself to others?

- What if you could accept yourself for who you are, flaws and all? And know that not only is it okay to have flaws, it also makes us interesting and human?

Social Media Exploration

5 minutes (exercise)
5 minutes (discussion)

Intention

- Explore students' usage of social media, including how they often compare themselves to others through social media

- Investigate how students feel when they compare themselves to others

Instructions

- Read the following script to students:

  Now, let's do a pen-and-paper exercise designed to explore our use of social media and the effects that these platforms have on us.

  Begin by closing your eyes, fully or partially, and taking a moment to check in, feeling the movement of the breath as it flows in and out of your body.

  How are you feeling right now? Please open your eyes and write down anything that is present.

  Now, I invite you to pull out your phone and open up your most-used social media app. Take a minute to scroll through, paying particular attention to how what you're seeing on the app makes you feel.

  Write down any feelings that come up while you're scrolling. For example:

    ○ *I feel unworthy.*

    ○ *I feel like I don't measure up.*

    ○ *I feel angry or sad.*

    ○ *I feel inspired.*

    ○ *I feel like I'm not good enough.*

    ○ *I feel entertained.*

    ○ *I feel lonely.*

  When you're ready, put your phone down, close your eyes, and place a hand over your heart or anywhere that feels soothing to you.

Then offer yourself compassion for any feelings of distress or unworthiness that may have arisen, perhaps saying to yourself:

- ○ *I wish to treat myself with kindness in this moment.*

- ○ *I hope to know that I am enough, just as I am.*

- ○ *What would I say to a good friend who was feeling this way?*

Now, ask yourself, "In what ways could I treat myself with more compassion when it comes to my social media usage?" Write down any ideas that come to mind.

How does scrolling through social media make you feel? Are there times when you feel more connected? Times when you feel less connected or more self-critical?

When you're ready, gently open your eyes if they've been closed.

Discussion

- What did you notice when you began scrolling through your social media today? Did you notice a change in how you felt from before you began scrolling?

- Were you able to offer yourself compassion for any self-criticism that arose?

2 minutes

Intention

- Reinforce skills learned in this session

Instructions

- Encourage students to practice 5 to 10 minutes of formal practice per day, in addition to practicing informally throughout the week.

- Students' choice! Students can choose anything from their toolkit for home practice.

Toolkit	
Informal Tools	**Formal Tools**
1. Supportive Gestures	1. Sunbathing
2. Good Friend Question (Ask yourself: How would I treat a friend?)	2. Compassionate Friend
3. Sound Practice	3. Compassionate Body Scan
4. Soles of the Feet	4. Affectionate Breathing
5. Mindful Eating	5. Kindness for Someone You Care About
6. Here-and-Now Stone	6. A Person Just Like Me
7. Three Soothing Breaths	7. Calming Music
8. Finding Kindness Phrases	8. Compassionate Letter Writing

Wrap-Up

- What will you take away from this session? [*Ask for a volunteer to start, and then go around the room, with each student offering something that stands out to them about this session. Give students the option to pass if they do not want to share. If time is limited, ask just a few students to respond.*]

 **SESSION 10**

Common Humanity

Session Overview

- *Opening Art Activity*: Japanese Bowl (10 min)

- *Practice Discussion* (5 min)

- *Exercise*: Crossing the Line (10 min)

- *Exercise*: Japanese Bowls (15 min)

- *Story*: A Cracked Pot (while completing the *Japanese Bowls* exercise)

- *Home Practice* (2 min)

In This Session, You Will . . .

- Demonstrate the concept of common humanity

- Explain how our "flaws" are not really flaws

Materials

- Paper or pressed-cardboard (not wax-covered) bowls

- Black pens

- Gold paint pens or gold permanent markers

- Rope

- YouTube video: "Peter Mayer Japanese Bowl"
  (https://www.youtube.com/watch?v=qOAzobTIGr8)

Japanese Bowl

10 minutes

Intention

- Help students transition from their regular class to self-compassion class by stilling and quieting the mind

- Preview the Japanese bowl concept that will be discussed later in the session

Instructions

- Give each student a bowl and a black pen.

- Turning the bowl upside down, ask students to draw sections on their bowls using the black pen and to create different designs or patterns in each section.

- Emphasize that the intention is not the quality of the artwork—it is the act of paying attention on purpose. For this reason, it is fine if students do not complete filling in all sections. They will likely not have time to do so.

- The bowls will be used later in the session.

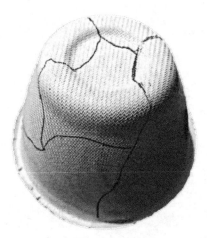
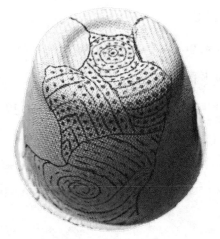

PRACTICE DISCUSSION

5 minutes

Intention

- Check in with students to see how their home practice is progressing

- Gently encourage practice by highlighting instances when self-compassion skills can be used

Instructions

- Ask students if they've encountered stressful moments over the past week, and invite them to share their experiences of using any of the practices they've learned. Example practices include:

  - *Soles of the Feet*

  - *Here-and-Now Stone*

  - *Finding Kindness Phrases*

  - *A Person Just Like Me*

  - *Calming Music*

- Ask them if they did any formal practice during the week and, if so, how that went for them. Remind them that formal practices help them to remember to do the informal practices.

- Are they beginning to see certain practices that are becoming favorites? Remind them that they do not have to do all the practices. They have a "buffet" of practices from which they can pick and choose their favorites.

- Were they able to create a playlist of relaxing instrumental music to use when they feel stressed?

- Are they continuing to ask themselves, "What words do I want to hear? What words would be most comforting and supportive to me?" Are they then incorporating those words into kindness phrases?

Crossing the Line

5 minutes (exercise)
5 minutes (discussion)

Intention

- Demonstrate common humanity and create deeper bonding in the group

Instructions

- Invite students to stand in a line.

- Hold a rope between yourself and the assistant (if available), or place the rope on the floor (if no assistant is available). If the rope is held between two people, it can be raised or lowered between each phrase to make "crossing the line" more engaging.

- Remind students to remain quiet during the practice in order to create safety, as this exercise requires vulnerability.

- Read each phrase slowly and ask students to "cross the line" (go to the other side of the rope) if the phrase applies to them. Pause after each phrase to give students time to cross the line. After each time students cross the line and all have observed, instruct others who have not crossed the line to join the others on the other side of the line.

- Cross the line if you have:

    o Been proud of an accomplishment

    o Felt rejected by a friend or a group

    o Been bullied

    o Felt frustrated or angry with parents

    o Felt pressured to perform or achieve by parents, teachers, or coaches

    o Felt alone

    o Felt rejected by others

    o Felt guilty about something you've done to someone else

    o Felt that you don't belong

- Compared yourself to an image in the media
- Compared your body image to your friends'
- Felt like you didn't measure up in some way
- Felt compassion when you saw an animal or a person suffering or hurt in some way

- When doing this exercise, periodically remind students to look around to observe the number of students crossing the line.

Discussion

- What did you notice while doing this exercise?
- What feelings were you aware of?
- How did you feel when you saw others cross the line with you?
- How would self-compassion be useful in any of these situations?

Japanese Bowls

10 minutes (exercise)
5 minutes (discussion)

Intention

- Provide a metaphor for reframing our flaws and imperfections as characteristics that make us uniquely human

Instructions

- Explain to students that the following video will illustrate the Japanese art form of *kintsugi*, in which broken pottery is repaired by mending together the broken pieces with gold lacquer, creating an even more beautiful and unique work of art.

- Show students "Peter Mayer Japanese Bowl" (https://www.youtube.com/watch?v=qOAzobTIGr8).

- Be sure to have time to discuss this video with teens. Some teens are ready to discuss how they have always seen their "cracks" as imperfections, which leads to self-criticism and low self-esteem. The video reminds them to find value in their flaws and instills the hope that they can fill their own cracks with gold (i.e., self-compassion).

- Once students finish the video and discuss its value, invite students back to the Japanese bowls they were working on at the beginning of the session.

- They can now use the gold markers to go over their cracks (i.e., the black lines) with gold.

- You can read the story on the following page while students go over their cracks with gold marker.

Discussion

- What would it be like to respect and honor the "damaged" parts of ourselves, or the parts of ourselves that we don't like?

- What are some ways that we can respect and honor the "damaged" parts of ourselves?

A Cracked Pot

*3 minutes (while students are drawing over the black lines
with gold marker in the Japanese Bowls exercise)*

Intention

- To emphasize that what we may consider are our flaws or imperfections is what may make us interesting to others

Instructions

- Read the following story to students as they finish their Japanese bowls:

  A water bearer in India had two large pots, one hung on each end of a pole, which she carried across her neck.

  One of the pots had a crack in it. While the other pot was perfect and always delivered a full portion of water at the end of the long walk from the stream to the house, the cracked pot arrived only half full.

  For a full two years this went on daily, with the bearer delivering only one and a half pots full of water to her house.

  The perfect pot was proud of its accomplishments, perfect to the end for which it was made. But the poor cracked pot was ashamed of its own imperfection and miserable that it was able to accomplish only half of what it had been made to do.

  After two years of what it perceived to be a bitter failure, it spoke to the water bearer one day by the stream: "I am ashamed of myself, and I want to apologize to you."

  "Why?" asked the bearer. "What are you ashamed of?"

  "I have been able, for these past two years, to deliver only half my load because this crack in my side causes water to leak out all the way back to your house. Because of my flaws, you have to do all of this work, and you don't get full value from your efforts," the pot said.

  The water bearer felt sorry for the old cracked pot, and in her compassion she said, "As we return to the house, I want you to notice the beautiful flowers along the path."

  Indeed, as they went up the hill, the old cracked pot took notice of the sun warming the beautiful wild flowers on the side of the path, and this cheered it some.

  But at the end of the trail, it still felt bad because it had leaked out half its load, and so again it apologized to the bearer for its failure.

The bearer said to the pot, "Did you notice that there were flowers only on your side of the path, but not on the other pot's side? That's because I have always known about your flaw, and I put it to good use. I planted flower seeds on your side of the path, and every day while we walk back from the stream, you've watered them. For two years, I have been able to pick these beautiful flowers to decorate my table. Without you being just the way you are, I would not have this beauty to grace my house."

The moral of the story? Each of us has our own unique flaws. We're all cracked pots.

But it's the cracks and flaws we each have that make our lives together so very interesting and rewarding. We've just got to take each person for what they are and look for the good in them.

There's a lot of good out there.

HOME PRACTICE

2 minutes

Intention

- Reinforce skills learned in this session

Instructions

- Encourage students to practice 5 to 10 minutes of formal practice per day, in addition to practicing informally throughout the week.

- Students' choice! They can choose anything from their toolkit for home practice.

Toolkit	
Informal Tools	**Formal Tools**
1. Supportive Gestures	1. Sunbathing
2. Good Friend Question (Ask yourself: How would I treat a friend?)	2. Compassionate Friend
3. Sound Practice	3. Compassionate Body Scan
4. Soles of the Feet	4. Affectionate Breathing
5. Mindful Eating	5. Kindness for Someone You Care About
6. Here-and-Now Stone	6. A Person Just Like Me
7. Three Soothing Breaths	7. Calming Music
8. Finding Kindness Phrases	8. Compassionate Letter Writing

Wrap-Up

- What will you take away from this session? [*Ask for a volunteer to start, and then go around the room, with each student offering something that stands out to them about this session. Give students the option to pass if they do not want to share. If time is limited, ask just a few students to respond.*]

 **SESSION 11**

Core Values

Session Overview

- *Opening Art Activity*: Mindful Frame (10 min)
- *Topic*: Core Values (5 min)
- *Exercise*: My House/My Self (25 min)
- *Home Practice* (2 min)

In This Session, You Will . . .

- Help students discover their core values—what gives their lives meaning in spite of their circumstances
- Teach students how we can reorient ourselves to those values in daily life

Materials

- Parchment paper (art paper that has been "antiqued")
- Black calligraphy pens
- Image of a house
- *My House/My Self Questions*
- *List of Core Values* (optional)

Mindful Frame

10 minutes

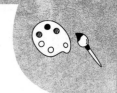

Intention

- Help students transition from their regular class to self-compassion class by stilling and quieting the mind

- Begin *A Pledge to Myself* art activity that will be completed in session 12

Instructions

- Give students a piece of "antique-looking" paper.

- Instruct them to create a border around the paper using any design that they would like. Ask them to leave the center of the "frame" blank. (It will be used in session 12.)

- Remind them to pay attention to the physical sensations when they are drawing—the feel of the pen in their hand, the pressure of their hand on the paper, the pressure of the pen on the paper.

- Whenever they notice their mind wandering, have them gently, and without judgment, bring their attention back to the physical sensations of drawing.

Core Values

5 minutes

Intention

- Help students understand the meaning of core values so they are better able to identify and give themselves what they need

Talking Points

- We can't give ourselves what we really need if we don't know what we value most in life. And what we value the most depends on our core values.

- Values are beliefs that guide how we live our lives. They are beliefs about what we feel is important to us.

- People often confuse the concept of values with goals. What do you think the difference is between goals and values?

    - Goals are destinations, while values point us in the direction to get there.

    - For this reason, goals can be achieved (they have a finish line), while values are beliefs that guide how we continually live out our lives.

- What are some examples of core values?

    - Education
    - Being a good friend
    - Family
    - Faith
    - Nature

    - Loyalty
    - Honesty
    - Being authentic
    - Doing your best

- When we know our core values, it becomes easier to give ourselves compassion because we know what we need.

Teaching Tip: (*optional*) You can give students the following *List of Core Values* if they have trouble coming up with their own core values.

List of Core Values

❑ Achievement	❑ Equality	❑ Leadership
❑ Adventure	❑ Excitement	❑ Learning
❑ Attentiveness	❑ Experience	❑ Love
❑ Authenticity	❑ Fairness	❑ Loyalty
❑ Authority	❑ Faith	❑ Meaning
❑ Autonomy	❑ Fame	❑ Nesting
❑ Balance	❑ Fitness	❑ Nurturance
❑ Beauty	❑ Flow	❑ Openness
❑ Belonging	❑ Forgiveness	❑ Optimism
❑ Boldness	❑ Freedom	❑ Order
❑ Caring	❑ Friendships	❑ Organization
❑ Challenge	❑ Fun	❑ Patience
❑ Citizenship	❑ Growth	❑ Peace
❑ Comfort	❑ Happiness	❑ Perseverance
❑ Communication	❑ Health	❑ Play
❑ Community	❑ Honesty	❑ Pleasure
❑ Compassion	❑ Honor	❑ Poise
❑ Competency	❑ Humor	❑ Popularity
❑ Connectedness	❑ Imagination	❑ Recognition
❑ Conservation	❑ Influence	❑ Reliability
❑ Contribution	❑ Inner harmony	❑ Reputation
❑ Creativity	❑ Integrity	❑ Respect
❑ Curiosity	❑ Intelligence	❑ Responsibility
❑ Detachment	❑ Intimacy	❑ Reverence
❑ Determination	❑ Intuition	❑ Rhythm
❑ Discipline	❑ Justice	❑ Risk
❑ Diversity	❑ Kindness	❑ Security
❑ Effort	❑ Knowledge	❑ Self-expression

My House/My Self

25 minutes

Intention

- Help students identify their core values and understand how to respond when they stray from what is important to them

- Understand the obstacles to core values

- Consider how self-compassion can be useful when students aren't able to live by their core values (and how self-compassion can help them live a life more aligned with their core values)

Instructions

- Provide students with a drawing of a house* and the following list of questions as a way to explore their core values:

  - Foundation: What things are foundational to you? What is most important to you?

  - Window: When you look out the window of your house into the future, what do you see?

  - Path to front door: What things lead you to your house (i.e., things you believe in)?

  - Garden: What kinds of things would you like to grow and cultivate in your life?

  - Inside the house: Who are the people who have influenced you in your life?

  - Mailbox: What parts of yourself would you like to send out into the world?

  - Fence: What are the things that you want to keep away from your house?

  - Roof: What keeps you inside your house? What is limiting you?

  - Bricks: What holds you together?

---

* In some communities, students may not live in houses. If this is the case for your students, feel free to offer a different image and adjust the questions accordingly, or you can skip using the image entirely. The image is merely intended to scaffold students' ability to visualize the different parts of the house so the metaphor is more accessible.

- Tell students to write out the answers to these questions on the drawing itself or a separate piece of paper. If they would like to add some other components to their house, they can feel free to do so.

- Explain that they may get the same or similar answers to several of the questions, and that's okay. They may also not have enough time to finish answering all the questions, and that's okay too. The point of the exercise is to get them thinking about their core values.

- With this exercise, it is very important that students have time to reflect on the questions. That is the only way that it works. Give students at least 10 minutes to complete the exercise.

- If time allows, ask students to pair up with someone and to take this person on a "tour" of their house. They can explain some or all of their values with their partner (as much or as little detail as they would like to share).

- Then come back to the large group and discuss obstacles to core values. Ask students:

  o What prevents you from living by your core values?

  o What would help you connect with and live more from your core values?

- Explain that there is a possibility that we can live in accordance with our core values, but we can also forgive ourselves when we don't live by them. For example, let's say that we stray from our core values by getting swept up with what our friends are doing and we end up acting in a way that we don't feel is healthy for us. Or someone mistreats us, and in the moment, we respond in a way that we're not proud of.

- In both of the above situations, we can forgive ourselves for straying from our core values. Through mindfulness—being aware of how we're feeling in the moment—we're better able to notice earlier that the situation is unhealthy, and through self-compassion, we're better able to stand up for ourselves and say that we don't want to engage in this activity, or we can more effectively express that we feel mistreated.

Teaching Tip: Peer pressure is often an obstacle for teens to live in accordance with their core values. Respond to this obstacle by helping teens recognize the conflict between living a life that is consistent with their core values versus being accepted by the group. Remind students that wanting to belong and be accepted by others is a natural human need. Encourage students to extend compassion to themselves while navigating this difficult conflict.

HOME PRACTICE
2 minutes

Intention

- Reinforce skills learned in this session

Instructions

- Encourage students to practice 5 to 10 minutes of formal practice per day, in addition to practicing informally throughout the week.

- Students' choice! They can choose anything from their toolkit for home practice.

Toolkit	
Informal Tools	**Formal Tools**
1. Supportive Gestures	1. Sunbathing
2. Good Friend Question (Ask yourself: How would I treat a friend?)	2. Compassionate Friend
3. Sound Practice	3. Compassionate Body Scan
4. Soles of the Feet	4. Affectionate Breathing
5. Mindful Eating	5. Kindness for Someone You Care About
6. Here-and-Now Stone	6. A Person Just Like Me
7. Three Soothing Breaths	7. Calming Music
8. Finding Kindness Phrases	8. Compassionate Letter Writing

Wrap-Up

- What will you take away from this session? [*Ask for a volunteer to start, and then go around the room, with each student offering something that stands out to them about this session. Give students the option to pass if they do not want to share. If time is limited, ask just a few students to respond.*]

 **SESSION 12**

Silver Linings

Session Overview

- *Opening Art Activity*: A Pledge to Myself (10 min)

- *Formal Practice*: Giving and Receiving Compassion (15 min)

- *Topic*: Finding Value in Our Struggles (5 min)

- *Exercise*: Silver Linings (15 min)

- *Home Practice* (2 min)

In This Session, You Will . . .

- Help students make a promise or pledge to help them
  live in accordance with their core values

- Remind students to forgive themselves when they stray
  from their core values (we're human, after all!)

Materials

- Antiqued paper frame from session 11

- Calligraphy pens

- Paper

- Pencils

- 18-inch pieces of ribbon

OPENING ART ACTIVITY

A Pledge to Myself

10 minutes

Intention

- Help students transition from their regular class to self-compassion class by stilling and quieting the mind

- Finish the *Mindful Frame* activity from session 11

Instructions

- In this exercise, have students choose one of their core values to make an intention, or pledge, that they can use to use to get back on track when they go astray in their lives. This promise is not an unbreakable contract but simply provides a way to reorient themselves and their behavior when they stray from what's important to them.

- To create this intention, ask students to make a wish for themselves that they would like to manifest each day. In the middle of the paper frame they created in the *Mindful Frame* activity from session 11, have them write this intention in the form of "I pledge to _____, as best I can."

- For example, if a student's value is music, their wish may be to spend more time playing guitar, resulting in the intention "I pledge to play the guitar each day, as best as I can."

- Encourage students to repeat this intention to themselves each morning when they get up or every night before they go to bed.

- They can also save the intention somewhere on their phone or use part of it as a password to access websites or apps.

- If time allows, students can continue working on the frame, decorating it whatever way they would like.

- Finally, if they would like, have students roll their paper frame into a scroll and tie it with a ribbon.

FORMAL PRACTICE

Giving and Receiving Compassion

10 minutes (practice)
5 minutes (inquiry)

Intention

- Cultivate the skill of giving compassion to others while simultaneously practicing self-compassion

Instructions

- Read the following script to students:

Please sit comfortably, closing your eyes if that feels right for you, and take a few deep, relaxing breaths, allowing yourself to feel the sensation of breathing in and breathing out, noticing how your breath energizes your body as you inhale and soothes your body as you exhale.

Letting your breathing find its own natural rhythm, continue feeling the sensation of breathing in and out. If you would like, put a hand over your heart or use another supportive gesture as a reminder to bring not just awareness but kind and supportive awareness to your experience and to yourself.

Now, focusing your attention on your in-breath, let yourself enjoy the sensation of breathing in, one breath after another, noticing how your in-breath nourishes every cell in your body.

If you wish, you can also carry a word on each in-breath, such as connected, safe, strength, *or* belonging, *giving yourself whatever you need in this moment.*

Now, call to mind someone to whom you would like to send warmth and kindness, either someone you love or someone who is struggling and needs compassion. Visualize this person clearly in your mind. Get a really good image of them—the expression on their face, maybe what they're wearing.

Shift your focus now to your out-breath, feeling your body breathe out and sending warmth and good wishes to this person with each exhalation.

If you would like, you can add a kind word with each out-breath, or an image, or just offer the comfort and ease of your exhalation.

Now, feel your body breathe both in and out, breathing in for yourself and breathing out for another. One for me, one for you. Just feel the breath now. One for me, one for you.

However you may be feeling, allow that feeling to be here, setting the intention to breathe kindness for yourself and another.

Allow your breathing to flow in and out like the gentle movement of the sea, flowing in and flowing out, letting yourself be a part of this limitless, boundless flow, breathing in and breathing out.

If you wish, you can focus a little more on yourself if you feel like you need more kindness. It isn't selfish to do that. Or you can focus on the other person if you prefer.

And as you breathe out, feel free to send love and compassion to other people, to groups of people, to the world in general.

When you're ready, gently open your eyes.

Inquiry

- What was it like to give compassion to yourself?

- What was it like to give compassion to others?

- Was it easier to give compassion to yourself or another?

Teaching Tip: If working with students with trauma, it is important to remind them that it is okay to keep their eyes open or to place a hand on the belly to help focus attention on the physical sensation of breathing. Remind students who have experienced trauma that it's fine to breathe in compassion and kindness for themselves without necessarily needing to focus on others. If a student with a history of trauma gets activated, invite them to sit up and focus on an external object, such as something on the opposite side of the room.

Finding Value in Our Struggles

5 minutes

Intention

- Help students discover that there is value in experiencing challenges and struggles in life

Talking Points

- While most of us are afraid of failing, failure is part of the human experience, and it's often where we learn lessons we wouldn't have learned otherwise.

- Challenges force us to go deep inside and discover resources and insights that we didn't know we had.

- There is an old expression that says, "Every cloud has a silver lining," meaning that even when a cloud is blocking the sun, we can still see glimmers of the sun peeking around behind it.

- It's the same with the difficult experiences we encounter in life. As hard as these situations may be, there is also the possibility that they hold some "silver linings"—that there are good aspects of it that may not be immediately apparent. We can learn from our struggles and challenges in life by looking for the value in what seems to be an overwhelmingly negative situation.

- It's also important to remember that sometimes it's really hard to see the silver lining, especially when we're right in the middle of the painful experience. Sometimes, it just feels like pain, with nothing positive. Sometimes, we need a lot of time following the painful experience in order to get perspective on it and see what we've learned from it.

- And when it feels like all-consuming pain or hurt, we can remember to give ourselves compassion. Continually. Remember, there's no shortage of compassion, and the more we give to ourselves, the more we'll have the resources to give to others.

Teacher Tip: Students are less likely to resent and resist suffering when they see the value in it. If possible, choose to offer a personal example of your own struggles that would be appropriate to share with students.

Silver Linings

10 minutes (exercise)
5 minutes (discussion)

Intention

- Identify a silver lining in a past event that was very difficult at the time yet offered some important life lesson

- Help students learn to turn toward emotional pain with curiosity

- Facilitate students in seeing that they can face emotional pain without falling apart

Instructions

- Read the following script to students:

Please think of a past struggle in your own life that seemed very difficult or even impossible at the time and that, looking back, you learned something important from that you wouldn't have learned otherwise. Please write this down.

What deeper lesson did the challenge or crisis teach you that you probably would never have learned otherwise? Please write that down too.

Can you think of a challenge that you are presently experiencing in your life that you might eventually find has a silver lining? Write this down also.

Discussion

- What did you learn from this exercise?

- How do you feel after completing this exercise?

- Could you find any way that the struggles that you might be experiencing now might be teaching you something that you'll benefit from later?

2 minutes

Intention

- Reinforce skills learned in this session

Instructions

- Encourage students to practice 5 to 10 minutes of formal practice per day, in addition to practicing informally throughout the week.

- New tool for the toolkit: *Giving and Receiving Compassion*

Toolkit	
Informal Tools	**Formal Tools**
1. Supportive Gestures	1. Sunbathing
2. Good Friend Question (Ask yourself: How would I treat a friend?)	2. Compassionate Friend
3. Sound Practice	3. Compassionate Body Scan
4. Soles of the Feet	4. Affectionate Breathing
5. Mindful Eating	5. Kindness for Someone You Care About
6. Here-and-Now Stone	6. A Person Just Like Me
7. Three Soothing Breaths	7. Calming Music
8. Finding Kindness Phrases	8. Compassionate Letter Writing
	9. Giving and Receiving Compassion

Wrap-Up

- What will you take away from this session? [*Ask for a volunteer to start, and then go around the room, with each student offering something that stands out to them about this session. Give students the option to pass if they do not want to share. If time is limited, ask just a few students to respond.*]

 **SESSION 13**

Getting to Know Difficult Emotions

Session Overview

- *Opening Art Activity*: Oobleck (15 min)

- *Formal Practice*: Noticing Sounds (10 min)

- *Topic*: Working with Difficult Emotions (5 min)

- *Informal Practice*: Soften, Support, Open (15 min)

- *Home Practice* (2 min)

In This Session, You Will . . .

- Show students how to work with difficult emotions by turning toward them rather than resisting them

Materials

- Oobleck

Oobleck

15 minutes

Intention

- Provide a visceral experience in preparation for the practice of *Soften, Support, Open*

Instructions

- When students arrive, provide them with a small handful of oobleck. (See below for recipe.) This is a substance made from cornstarch and water, and it has properties similar to both solids and liquids. When it is held tightly in your hand, it is like a solid. When you open your hand, it becomes runny, like a liquid.

- Invite students to play with this substance, making sure they observe what happens when they roll the oobleck into a ball (i.e., it becomes firm) versus what happens when they then open their hand (i.e., it flattens, oozes, and may become runny).

Recipe

- Be sure to prepare the oobleck in advance and store it in a sealed container.

- Mix one part water with roughly two parts cornstarch. You may wish to start with one cup of water and one and a half cups of cornstarch, then work in more cornstarch if you want a more solid oobleck.

- It will take about five minutes of mixing to get nice homogeneous oobleck. Its consistency should be such that you can roll it into a semifirm ball, but when you open your hand, it "melts" into a flat pancake.

- When you get close to the right consistency, add only a few drops of water at a time.

- Oobleck should always be stored in a closed container to reduce the likelihood of it drying out. If it dries out, it may require a bit of water to restore its original consistency.

Teaching Tip: Although oobleck cleans up easily, it's best to cover surfaces or give students a paper plate or paper towel to keep underneath it. The purpose of playing with oobleck is for students to get a visceral experience of what happens when they hold something tightly (i.e., it becomes hard) versus when they allow something to just be (i.e., it softens). Although most students love playing with oobleck, there may be a student who doesn't feel comfortable touching this substance. It's fine for them not to participate, but invite them to observe what happens when others play with it.

Noticing Sounds

5 minutes (practice)
5 minutes (inquiry)

Intention

- Cultivate the mindfulness skill of listening

- Allow students to settle after the activating experience of playing with oobleck

Instructions

- Read the following script to students:

Please sit comfortably, closing your eyes if that feels okay for you, and take a few deep, relaxing breaths, allowing yourself to feel the sensation of breathing in and breathing out, noticing how your breath nourishes your body as you inhale and soothes your body as you exhale.

Letting your breathing find its own natural rhythm, continue feeling the sensation of breathing in and breathing out. If you would like, you can use a supportive gesture to remind yourself to be gentle and kind to yourself in this moment and always.

Now, bring your attention to the sounds around you, including sounds that are nearby (here in your classroom) and sounds that are farther away (maybe outside your classroom). What do you hear? [long pause]

If there is a sound that is pleasant to you, can you open to it? Allow it to wash over you? Allow yourself to really hear it?

Is there a sound that might be unpleasant, a sound that perhaps is annoying to you? If so, can you turn toward that sound? Allow yourself to really hear it? In other words, can you really pay attention to it?

Now, bring your attention back to your breath, noticing your inhale and your exhale, all the way from the beginning of your in-breath through to the end of your out-breath.

When you're ready, gently open your eyes if they've been closed.

Inquiry

- What did you notice when you listened to sounds?

- What happened when you really paid attention to the pleasant sounds?

- What happened when you really paid attention to the unpleasant sounds?

- How did it feel when you turned toward the unpleasant sound? [*Accept all responses—students may say that often it is not as unpleasant as they thought.*]

Working with Difficult Emotions

5 minutes

Intention

- Give teens tools to deal with difficult emotions

Talking Points

- How many of you have ever felt anger? Fear? Worry? Grief? And when you feel these difficult emotions, how do you generally deal with them? What are some typical ways you react to or try to manage challenging emotions?

- Today, we are going to talk about three helpful strategies to deal with these difficult emotions:
  - Labeling emotions
  - Finding emotions in the body
  - Soften, support, open

Labeling Emotions

- The first step in managing a strong or difficult emotion is to label or name it.

- When we name these emotions, we actually engage the part of the brain that helps us to think clearly, called the prefrontal cortex, which then communicates with the amygdala, which is part of the limbic system and is the part of the brain responsible for emotions.

- When we say, "This is anger" or "This is hurt," we begin to calm the excited, over-stimulated amygdala, which is responsible for these painful feelings.

- When we turn toward our strong emotions in this way, we actually develop a new relationship to them. This is how we "unstick" ourselves from the story in our heads that is promoting these strong emotions. By naming these emotions, we can tame them. There is a phrase that can help us remember this step: "Name it to tame it."

- The voice that we use to label our emotions also makes a difference. It's helpful to use a kind, gentle voice, which allows the amygdala to deactivate a little. Notice the tone of voice that you use.

Finding Emotions in the Body

- The next step is to mindfully notice where you are experiencing a strong or difficult emotion. All emotions have a physical component, which is experienced as a sensation in the body.

- For example, when we're angry, we might feel physical tension in the abdomen as the body prepares for a fight.

- Sometimes it's difficult to identify strong emotions—thoughts are very fast and we usually can't catch them—but the body is slow, so if we focus our attention on the experience of physical sensations, we can more easily locate and identify our emotions. And when we can locate and anchor these emotions, they start to change!

- There is another phrase that can remind us to find where emotions live in the body: "Feel it and you heal it."

- A difficult emotion changes even more when we establish a loving, accepting relationship to it, so if we can bring awareness in with a kinder and more accepting tone, it becomes safer to feel it.

Soften, Support, Open

- The last step is to practice soften, support, open, which is a compassionate response to difficult emotions we may find in the body.

- After we find where in the body the difficult emotion resides, we can **soften** that area—imagining that it is relaxing a little—giving it space to perhaps "melt" a little. In other words, if it were a tight ball, the tight ball might relax and become more spacious—kind of what happens when a dry sponge is put in water.

- **Support** happens when we provide a physical comforting gesture to ourselves—a show of support. We can also say some kind and encouraging words to ourselves.

- Finally, **open** is about giving this emotion space to simply be. So often, we tend to run away from difficult emotions because, let's face it, they aren't easy to feel. So we might hide from them or resist them, pushing them away. "Open" simply means that we let go, or let the emotion be, as much as we are able. For example, we can imagine widening the space where the emotion is in the body so that it has lots of room to just be there.

INFORMAL PRACTICE

Soften, Support, Open

10 minutes (practice)
5 minutes (discussion)

Intention

- Provide mindfulness and self-compassion techniques for working with difficult emotions

Instructions

- Read the following script to students:

The following practice is a combination of three informal practices we can use to name and tame strong emotions any time we become aware of difficulty. This can be done as an informal on-the-spot practice. Each component can be done separately or together.

To begin, please find a comfortable position, close your eyes if that feels right to you, and take three relaxing breaths. Place your hand on your heart or give yourself another supportive gesture to remind yourself that you are in the room and to bring kindness to yourself.

Now, let yourself recall a mild to moderately difficult situation that you are experiencing in your life right now, perhaps a problem you are having with a friend or parent, maybe someone in trouble you feel worried about, or a problem in school (like feeling bullied, left out, or unappreciated). It's best not to choose the most difficult problem you are dealing with, or a tiny problem that doesn't cause much stress. You want to choose a problem that can generate a little stress in your body when you think of it.

Clearly visualize this situation. Who was there? What was said? What happened? Try to get a good image of this situation in your mind.

Labeling Emotions

Now that you're thinking about this situation, see if you can name the different emotions that arise within you. Anger? Sadness? Grief? Confusion? Fear? Loneliness? Frustration?

If a couple different emotions are arising, see if you can name the strongest emotion—a difficult emotion—associated with that situation.

Repeat the name of the emotion to yourself in a gentle, understanding voice, as if you were validating a friend's feelings: "That's hurt," "That's sadness," or "That's embarrassment."

Use the same warmhearted tone of voice that you would use if you were validating how a friend feels. If you said to your friend, "Wow, I can see you're really feeling bad," what tone of voice would you use? Use this same voice with yourself right now.

Finding Emotions in the Body

Now, expand your awareness to your body as a whole.

Recall the difficult situation again and scan your body for where you feel it the most. In your mind's eye, sweep your body from head to toe, stopping where you sense a little tension or discomfort.

Now, choose a single location in your body where the feeling seems to be the strongest. Perhaps you notice a tense muscle or achy feeling, like a heartache, or a burning or gripping in your stomach, chest, or throat. Notice how that feels right now.

If you just want to acknowledge that the sensations are there but don't want to work with them, just naming the sensations can be helpful. You can take your time working with the sensations in the body.

Soften, Support, Open

Now, soften around this area where you feel the sensation in your body, letting the muscles soften as if applying heat to sore muscles. Recall the way the oobleck softened in your hands. You can say quietly to yourself, "Soft, soft" and imagine the sensation softening just like the oobleck did. Remember that you are not trying to make the sensation go away—you are just holding it softly, like the way you might hold a baby chick, very delicately and with tenderness.

And now, offer a little support for yourself just because you have been struggling in this way with this strong emotion. Put your hand over your heart and feel your body breathe. Perhaps even add some kind words, such as "You've got this" or "I know I'm not the only person who has ever felt this way."

And now, open to the strong emotion or sensation that's here. Can you let go of the wish for it to go away or for the feeling to disappear? This is like what happened when you opened your hand when the oobleck was in it. It sort of relaxed and melted a little bit, didn't it? This is what you're trying to do—just opening up and allowing whatever feelings are there to just be there and maybe loosen up a bit.

If you experience too much discomfort with an emotion, you can always simply stay with your breath until you feel better.

You can repeat these three words—"Soften, support, open"—kind of like a favorite slogan or saying, reminding you to offer yourself a little kindness and warmth in these moments of difficulty or struggle.

Slowly open your eyes when you're ready.

Discussion

- Did you notice a change when you labeled the emotion associated with the situation?

- Were you able to find where it was located in your body?

- Did you notice that your emotional discomfort changed in any way when you explored your body for the physical sensation associated with the emotion?

- Did the emotion change when you softened that part of the body, supported yourself, and opened to it being there?

2 minutes

Intention

- Reinforce skills learned in this session

Instructions

- Encourage students to practice 5 to 10 minutes of formal practice per day, in addition to practicing informally throughout the week.

- As students go through the week, ask them to create a "Moment of Joy" list by keeping an eye out for things that make them smile. This can be things that strike them as beautiful, moving, "cool" looking, or funny—or just things that are pleasing to them for whatever reason. Let students know that they will be using this list in session 15.

- Or, if students would like, they can take a photo of these moments on their phones and create a folder of "Moments of Joy."

- New tools for the toolkit: *Noticing Sounds; Soften, Support, Open*

Toolkit	
Informal Tools	**Formal Tools**
1. Supportive Gestures	1. Sunbathing
2. Good Friend Question (Ask yourself: How would I treat a friend?)	2. Compassionate Friend
3. Sound Practice	3. Compassionate Body Scan
4. Soles of the Feet	4. Affectionate Breathing
5. Mindful Eating	5. Kindness for Someone You Care About
6. Here-and-Now Stone	6. A Person Just Like Me
7. Three Soothing Breaths	7. Calming Music
8. Finding Kindness Phrases	8. Compassionate Letter Writing
9. Soften, Support, Open	9. Giving and Receiving Compassion
	10. Noticing Sounds

Wrap-Up

- What will you take away from this session? [*Ask for a volunteer to start, and then go around the room, with each student offering something that stands out to them about this session. Give students the option to pass if they do not want to share. If time is limited, ask just a few students to respond.*]

 **SESSION 14**

Anger and the Adolescent Brain

Session Overview

- *Opening Art Activity*: Egg Writing (10 min)
- *Practice Discussion* (5 min)
- *Topic*: The Adolescent Brain (10 min)
- *Topic*: Working with Anger (5 min)
- *Informal Practice*: Exploring Unmet Needs (15 min)
- *Home Practice* (2 min)

In This Session, You Will . . .

- Deepen students' understanding of the biological basis of emotions in adolescence
- Introduce tools to manage difficult emotions when they arise

Materials

- Colored pencils
- Hardboiled eggs with the shell still on
- Plastic knives
- YouTube video: "Why the Teenage Brain Has an Evolutionary Advantage" (https://www.youtube.com/watch?v=P629TojpvDU) (*optional*)

Egg Writing

10 minutes

Intention

- Help students transition from their regular class to self-compassion class by stilling and quieting the mind

- Foreshadow the topic of *Working with Anger* and the practice of *Exploring Unmet Needs*

Instructions

- Provide each student with a hardboiled egg (with the shell still on).

- Ask them to think of things that make them angry and have them write these things on the shell of the egg using colored pencils.

- While students are doing this, guide them to notice the thoughts, feelings, and accompanying physical sensations that are arising.

- As thoughts arise, instruct students to notice these thoughts, acknowledge them, and allow them to "float" away by coming back to the physical sensations of the pencil in their hand, the feeling of the egg in their hand, and so forth.

- If it's helpful, they can imagine that these thoughts are like clouds in the sky that float into awareness, stay around for a bit, and then float out.

Teaching Tip: This art activity may be activating for some students as they recall things that make them angry. If you notice agitation in any students, use this as an opportunity to first acknowledge what they are feeling and then bring in a self-compassion practice, such as *Supportive Gestures*, or a mindfulness practice, such as *Soles of the Feet*.

PRACTICE DISCUSSION

5 minutes

Intention

- Check in with students on how home practice (both formal and informal) is progressing

Instructions

- Invite teens to share their experiences of the new home practices during the past week, and of mindfulness and self-compassion practice in general. You might ask them:

  ○ Has anyone had the opportunity to try out *Noticing Sounds*? If so, what was that like? How does it compare to *Calming Music*? Which do you prefer? The really nice thing about *Noticing Sounds* is that you can do it anytime and anywhere—on the school bus, outside in your backyard or on a park bench, even here at school!

  ○ How about *Soften, Support, Open*? Did anyone try that out? Remember, you don't have to do the whole practice. You can simply name the emotion—that helps to "unstick" it and gives you some perspective from the emotion.

  ○ I'm also curious about something—did anyone happen to make oobleck at home? Just for fun?

  ○ As a reminder, in addition to trying out the new practices, I encourage you to keep doing the practices from previous weeks that you liked and that worked for you. For example, *Soles of the Feet* is one that you can do anywhere without anyone even knowing. And many students really like *Calming Music*. So keep doing the ones that are helpful to you and that you enjoy.

- Check in with students regarding any challenges or obstacles they are running into, and ask if they have been able to access the prerecorded practices.

TOPIC

The Adolescent Brain

10 minutes

Intention

- Promote the understanding that many of the emotional highs and lows of adolescence have physiological explanations that are the result of developmental changes occurring in the brain

Talking Points

- The brain is going through many changes in adolescence. There are two brain areas in particular that are developing during this time—the prefrontal cortex and the limbic system.

- To help visualize these parts of the brain, make a fist with your thumb inside. The thumb represents the limbic system, while the front of your fingers represents the prefrontal cortex. [*For more detailed explanations, you can show students the following YouTube videos.*]

  - Dr. Dan Siegel's Hand Model of the Brain: https://www.youtube.com/watch?v=f-m2YcdMdFw

  - Dan Siegel—The Adolescent Brain: https://www.youtube.com/watch?v=0O1u5OEc5eY

  - Dan Siegel—Flipping Your Lid: A Scientific Explanation: https://www.youtube.com/watch?v=G0T_2NNoC68

- The limbic system, including the amygdala, is responsible for our emotions. If we suddenly feel sad and have the urge to cry, this is our limbic system at work. This experience of your emotions that you're having now is probably different from what it was a few years ago when you didn't have these huge shifts in your emotions from one minute to the next.

- The prefrontal cortex is responsible for logical thinking, planning, and decision-making. This is the part of the brain that helps us solve problems, think clearly, and control our impulses.

- These two parts of the brain grow at different rates. While they both start forming around age 11 or 12, the limbic system is generally completely developed by age 15, while the prefrontal cortex does not become fully developed until around age 25. [*For a greater visual representation, draw the following diagram on the whiteboard.*]

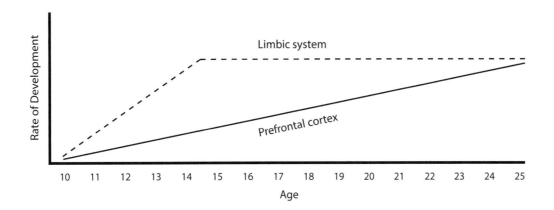

- We can think of this like being in a car that has a fully functioning accelerator (limbic system) and little brake action (prefrontal cortex). Your emotions are heightened, but you can't yet think through things as carefully as you will be able to later in life.

- Can you think of times when you felt like your emotions were out of whack in comparison to your logical thinking? When your accelerator was revved up without any brakes to slow it down?

- How did this feel to you? What was it like? How did you feel about yourself when it was all over?

- What can you do with the knowledge that your emotions during your teen years are often heightened? How can you work to ease some of these powerful emotions?

- What mindfulness practice does is give us more "brake" action by giving us the opportunity to pause before reacting.

- [*Show students "Why the Teenage Brain Has an Evolutionary Advantage" (https://www .youtube.com/watch?v=P629TojpvDU) (optional). Show the first 1:40 minutes only. This reinforces the explanation you just provided with a bit of humor.*]

Working with Anger

5 minutes

Intention

- Explore the usefulness of anger

- Become aware that there are "softer" feelings beneath the "hard" feeling of anger

- Recognize that there are often unmet needs underneath the softer feelings

Talking Points

- One of the strongest emotions that we often feel is anger, which we think of as a "hard" emotion.

- Although people often describe anger as a "bad" emotion, it has some positive functions, like all emotions. How do you think anger can be useful? [*Make sure to explain that anger gives us information, helps keep us safe, and motivates us to take action when a situation is unjust.*]

- How can anger be harmful? [*Make sure to explain that anger can lead to violence, it can perpetuate negative feelings, and it can be bad for relationships if not expressed skillfully.*]

- But if we continually harden our emotions in an attempt to protect ourselves against attack, we may become bitter and resentful over time. These are hard feelings.

- Often, underneath the hard feeling of anger are softer feelings that we are trying to cover up or protect ourselves from. These feelings may include fear, disappointment, hurt, or loneliness.

- Take out the hardboiled egg that you wrote on earlier. The outer shell is your anger. If you peel away the outer shell, what do you find inside? [*Have students peel away the outer shell.*] You'll notice that you find a white part, which represents the softer feelings that the shell was protecting.

- Now break your egg open or use the plastic knife to cut it in half. Inside you find the yolk. This is what you really need, that maybe you weren't getting, that made you feel hurt and then angry. We call these "unmet needs."

- Can you think of any unmet needs that you have that were underneath the soft feelings? [*Accept all answers. Possibilities include the need to belong, be accepted, be loved, be part of the group, be recognized for their value, etc.*]

Teaching Tip: Teens can get stuck with thoughts like "I don't think I can ever trust that friend again" or "How do I forgive someone who hurt me like that?" If they get swept up in the "story" of their situation, gently remind them that you are simply asking them to recognize the feeling—the hurt, sorrow, or sadness—beneath the anger and the unmet need as a way of learning to meet their own needs with kindness. Revisiting the "story" will cause the feeling to be regenerated and refueled.

Exploring Unmet Needs

10 minutes (practice)
5 minutes (discussion)

Intention

- Help students let go of anger that is no longer serving them

- Identify unmet needs underlying anger

- Practice self-compassion so students can meet some of their unmet needs

Instructions

- Read the following script to students:

This practice can bring up strong feelings. If you're feeling particularly sensitive today, feel free to skip this practice. If you decide to do it, please remember that you can change your mind at any point if you start to feel that it's bringing up stronger feelings than you want to deal with right now. If that happens, you can stop doing the exercise entirely and think about something else, like what's for lunch. Or you can simply focus on feeling your breath as you breathe in and out, think about the feeling of your feet on the floor, or give yourself a supportive gesture like holding one hand in the other. Remember that you are always in charge of your comfort and safety!

Please close your eyes if that feels right to you and think of a time that makes you feel angry, but not the most intense anger you've ever felt. Choose a situation where you feel like the anger is not helping you anymore, and you're ready to let it go. For example, you might be holding on to anger at a friend for something they did a while ago, but perhaps now you can see how this anger is just getting in the way. Give yourself a moment to think about this situation.

Know that it's completely natural for you to feel whatever way you do as you bring this situation to mind. Perhaps say to yourself, "Of course you're angry in a situation like this! Who wouldn't be?"

Sometimes we hold on to anger because we don't want to feel other feelings—feelings that make us feel more vulnerable. Consider that perhaps there are other feelings that the anger is covering up. What softer feelings might the anger be covering up? Maybe hurt? Disappointment? Sadness? Loneliness? Fear?

See if you can identify the softer feeling underlying the anger and allow yourself to name it. You can simply say to yourself something like "I was feeling lonely! That's what it was" or "I was afraid, and there is nothing wrong with that. Fear is a normal human emotion!"

And now, consider for a moment what you might have needed in this situation. What was it that you needed that you didn't get? Maybe to be noticed? To be appreciated? To be loved? To be accepted? To belong? Whatever you are feeling is quite natural. All teens—and adults too—have those needs!

If you'd like, put your hand over your heart and say some kind words to yourself because these feelings have surfaced, because you are human—not to make the feelings go away. Trust that the feelings will dissipate when the time is right.

If you are having trouble thinking of kind words to say to yourself, consider what you would say to a good friend who was having these same needs. Can you say these same words to yourself?

Perhaps you can even meet your deepest needs directly. For example, if you feel unloved, can you tell yourself "I love you"? If you feel unseen, can you tell yourself "I see you"? If you feel alone, can you tell yourself "I'm here for you"?

In other words, can you give to yourself right now what you've been hoping to receive from others? Can you say the words to yourself that you are most wanting to hear? And can you say them again and again?

And now, gently open your eyes.

Discussion

- How did it feel to validate your anger?

- Could you find the more vulnerable feelings underneath the anger?

- Were you able to identify the unmet need underneath the softer, more vulnerable feelings? Could you directly meet that need, even just a little?

- Did any struggles come up for you when doing this practice?

- How do you feel now?

HOME PRACTICE

2 minutes

Intention

- Reinforce skills learned in this session

Instructions

- Encourage students to practice 5 to 10 minutes of formal practice per day, in addition to practicing informally throughout the week.

- When students notice moments of anger over the next week, encourage them to ask themselves: What are the softer feelings beneath the anger? What are the unmet needs underneath these softer feelings?

- Ask students to continue practicing any of the informal or formal practices they've learned that work for them.

- Remind students that they will need their "Moments of Joy" photos or lists for the next session.

- New tool for the toolkit: *Exploring Unmet Needs*

Toolkit	
Informal Tools	**Formal Tools**
1. Supportive Gestures	1. Sunbathing
2. Good Friend Question (Ask yourself: How would I treat a friend?)	2. Compassionate Friend
3. Sound Practice	3. Compassionate Body Scan
4. Soles of the Feet	4. Affectionate Breathing
5. Mindful Eating	5. Kindness for Someone You Care About
6. Here-and-Now Stone	6. A Person Just Like Me
7. Three Soothing Breaths	7. Calming Music
8. Finding Kindness Phrases	8. Compassionate Letter Writing
9. Soften, Support, Open	9. Giving and Receiving Compassion
10. Exploring Unmet Needs (Ask yourself: What's beneath the anger?)	10. Noticing Sounds

Wrap-Up

- What will you take away from this session? [*Ask for a volunteer to start, and then go around the room, with each student offering something that stands out to them about this session. Give students the option to pass if they do not want to share. If time is limited, ask just a few students to respond.*]

SESSION 15

Embracing Your Life with Gratitude

Session Overview

- *Opening Art Activity*: Things That Make You Smile (10 min)

- *Topic*: Negativity Bias (5 min)

- *Formal Practice*: Calming Music (10 min)

- *Topic*: Gratitude (10 min)

- *Exercise*: Finding Gratitude (10 min)

- *Home Practice* (2 min)

In This Session, You Will . . .

- Help students cultivate gratitude for the things, people, and experiences in their lives

Materials

- Paper

- Pencils

- Instrumental music (e.g., "Meditation and Yoga Music": https://www.youtube.com/watch?v=ndGtoUN1rPg)

- YouTube videos:

    - "The Science of Gratitude" (https://www.youtube.com/watch?v=JMd1CcGZYwU)

    - "Why Are Our Thoughts Often So Negative?" (https://www.youtube.com/watch?v=0BF1hJaNtms&t=1)

    - "Gratitude: The Short Film by Louie Schwartzberg" (https://www.youtube.com/watch?v=96hE_1CRxj4) (*optional*)

OPENING ART ACTIVITY

Things That Make You Smile

10 minutes

Intention

- Demonstrate to teens that they can capture "moments of joy" in their lives simply by paying attention mindfully and thoughtfully

- Help teens recognize that these moments are around us at all times and can be easily accessed simply by taking the time to notice them

Instructions

- Ask students to bring their "Moments of Joy" photos (or lists) from session 13 to class.

  - Students with photos can email one of their photos to you (so you can show them to the class on a large computer screen), or they can simply use their phone to share their photo with the class.

- Students with lists can share one moment of joy aloud. If they notice a pattern in the things that made them smile (e.g., their pets, friends, being outdoors), they can share that as well.

- Depending on the size of the group and amount of time available, several students will have time to share their moments of joy. They can share what about the moment made them smile and how they feel now when they are looking at these photos.

Teaching Tip: Make sure that students notice that when they revisit their photos or lists, they generally smile and are happy—and others in the room are often smiling as well. Explain to students that by making a conscious effort to notice those things that bring us joy, we can bring positive feelings into our lives as well as the lives of others.

Negativity Bias

5 minutes

Intention

- Introduce the concept that we have a biological inclination to remember the negative things that happen in our lives rather than the positive ones

- Help students understand that their negative moods or tendency to focus on negative events may be, in part, a result of our human "negativity bias"

Talking Points

- We have moments in our lives that are inspiring, exciting, fun, and that bring us a lot of joy.

- And we have the opportunity to savor these moments—to linger with them, to take them in, and to really enjoy them—so these moments are here all the time in front of us.

- But why don't we do that more often? Why do we tend to notice all the bad stuff that happens in our lives and not all the good stuff?

- We have what's called a "negativity bias," which means that we remember the negative stuff rather than the positive. This bias is an inherited tendency that was passed down to us from our ancestors over 150,000 years ago. Back then, our ancestors were hunting and had to be on the constant lookout for predators that could hurt them. The negativity bias allowed them to survive by helping them pay attention to potential threats in their environment. Those who were simply enjoying the beauty around them and weren't on the lookout were eaten by predators.

- That means we've inherited the genes of ancestors who were constantly aware of what could harm them. All of this is to say that we're hardwired for survival, not for happiness.

- [*Show students "Why Are Our Thoughts Often So Negative?" (https://www.youtube.com /watch?v=0BF1hJaNtms&t=1).*]

- This session is about learning how to make a switch—how to get in the habit of engaging in those things that bring us joy. The first step we've already learned, which is savoring. This is about noticing the things that make us smile and really taking them in.

- There are two more things that we'll be learning about—gratitude and self-appreciation.

Calming Music

5 minutes (practice)
5 minutes (inquiry)

Intention

- Allow teens to soothe themselves while mindfully listening to music

- Reinforce music as a formal mindfulness practice (as teens tend to really enjoy this practice)

Instructions

- Begin to play a piece of relaxing and soothing instrumental music, such as "Meditation and Yoga Music" (https://www.youtube.com/watch?v=ndGtoUN1rPg).

- Let students know they can put their heads on their desks while listening to the music.

- Instruct them to pay attention to the tones and sounds of the music, perhaps noticing the individual instruments.

- Whenever their mind begins to wander, guide students to bring their attention back to the tones of the music. Remind students of this periodically throughout the piece of music.

Inquiry

- How does your body feel after this practice?

- What did you do when you noticed your mind wandering? Were you able to bring it back to the tones of the music?

- Did you observe any self-judgment when you noticed your mind was wandering?

- What were your reactions to the music?

Gratitude

10 minutes

Intention

- Enhance teens' understanding of gratitude and how it lifts mood and engenders a sense of common humanity

Talking Points

- When we practice gratitude, it means that we appreciate the good things that life has given us. If we just focus on what we want but don't have, we'll remain in a negative state of mind.

- Here is a video explaining the science of gratitude. [*Show students "The Science of Gratitude" (https://www.youtube.com/watch?v=JMd1CcGZYwU).*]

- A great deal of research has shown that gratitude is related to better overall well-being, both physical well-being and mental well-being. For example, gratitude is linked with reduced chronic pain and lower blood pressure, and also with lower depression and more satisfaction with life.

- Gratitude can be practiced in a variety of ways. It's simply a habit that can be easily developed.

- How can you integrate an attitude of gratitude into your life? How can you remember to be grateful for what you have?

- Some ways are to look for gratitude apps (you can find several in the app store on your phone) or write down three things that you're grateful for each day before going to bed.

- In fact, research has shown that writing down three good things a day for two weeks increases happiness and reduces depression—more than taking Prozac (Sexton & Adair, 2019)!

- [*If time allows, you may also want to show students "Gratitude: The Short Film by Louie Schwartzberg" (https://www.youtube.com/watch?v=96hE_1CRxj4).*]

Finding Gratitude

5 minutes (exercise)
5 minutes (discussion)

Intention

- Bring the practice of gratitude into conscious awareness through writing

- Notice the effect that practicing gratitude has on emotions

Instructions

- Read the following script to students:

    What are you grateful for in your life? For one minute, write down all the things that come to mind that you are grateful for.

    Don't forget the little things, like a bottle of water, your favorite phone app, jellybeans, zippers, Velcro, or your favorite tennis shoes.

    Don't lift your pen off the paper for one minute—keep writing! If you can't think of anything for a moment, keep writing the same thing over and over until something comes to you.

- After one minute, invite students to share one or two things that they are grateful for to the large group. They can do this "popcorn style."

Discussion

- How do you feel now compared to before this exercise began? [*You'll find that students describe feeling happier, more contented, and more fulfilled.*] That's the power of gratitude—the ability to generate positive emotions!

2 minutes

Intention

- Reinforce skills learned in this session

Instructions

- Encourage students to practice 5 to 10 minutes of formal practice per day, in addition to practicing informally throughout the week.

- Each day, ask them to write down three things that they are grateful for. This should take no more than a few minutes.

- Have them also notice things that make them smile throughout the week and spend time with them—savor them!

- New tools for the toolkit: *Savoring; Gratitude*

Toolkit	
Informal Tools	**Formal Tools**
1. Supportive Gestures	1. Sunbathing
2. Good Friend Question (Ask yourself: How would I treat a friend?)	2. Compassionate Friend
3. Sound Practice	3. Compassionate Body Scan
4. Soles of the Feet	4. Affectionate Breathing
5. Mindful Eating	5. Kindness for Someone You Care About
6. Here-and-Now Stone	6. A Person Just Like Me
7. Three Soothing Breaths	7. Calming Music
8. Finding Kindness Phrases	8. Compassionate Letter Writing
9. Soften, Support, Open	9. Giving and Receiving Compassion
10. Exploring Unmet Needs (Ask yourself: What's beneath the anger?)	10. Noticing Sounds
11. Savoring (Notice things that make you smile and savor them)	11. Gratitude (Write down three things that you're grateful for each day)

Wrap-Up

- What will you take away from this session? [*Ask for a volunteer to start, and then go around the room, with each student offering something that stands out to them about this session. Give students the option to pass if they do not want to share. If time is limited, ask just a few students to respond.*]

SESSION 16

Maintaining the Practice

Session Overview

- *Opening Art Activity*: Creating Writing Paper (10 min)

- *Formal Practice*: Compassionate Friend (10 min)

- *Topic*: Self-Appreciation (5 min)

- *Exercise*: What Would I Like to Remember? (15 min)

- *Closing*: Sharing Thoughts (5 min)

In This Session, You Will . . .

- Wrap up the curriculum and reflect on what was meaningful to students throughout the program

Materials

- Bell or chime

- Pens

- Paper

- Crayons, markers, and colored pencils

- Envelopes

- Scissors

- List of practices from the toolkit

Creating Writing Paper

10 minutes

Intention

- Help teens transition from their regular class to self-compassion class by stilling and quieting the mind

- Practice mindfulness by bringing awareness to sensations, thoughts, and feelings when creating a personalized letter

- Create a personalized frame for the letter they will write later in the session

Instructions

- Give students an 8½" × 11" piece of paper and explain that later in the session, they will use it to write a letter.

- Instruct students to fold the paper lengthwise. Then ask them to use scissors to cut a design around the outer edges of the paper (not the folded edge) so that when the paper is opened, it has a "frame" that is symmetrical.

- Alternatively, students can use whatever art supplies are provided (e.g., crayons, markers, colored pencils) to create a border for their paper.

- As with the previous art activities, guide students to bring their awareness to the sensations of the writing utensil in their hand, the feeling of the paper on the desk, and any thoughts that might be arising.

- If students have any judgmental thoughts (like "Oooh, I like the design that my friend is creating better than mine"), have them simply note these thoughts and allow them to drift away. You can also guide students to say a few kind words to themselves (e.g., "It must be hard to hear those words") or to use a soothing gesture when these thoughts arise.

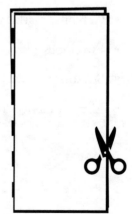

Compassionate Friend

5 minutes (practice)
5 minutes (inquiry)

Intention

- Show teens that they have a compassionate voice within themselves

- Help teens understand that they are capable of directing this compassionate voice toward themselves

Instructions

- This is the same practice that students already completed in session 1. Read the following script to students:

Begin by taking a few deep inhalations, allowing your shoulders to relax away from your ears. If you'd like to fold your arms and put your head down on your desk, feel free to do that. You can close your eyes if that's okay with you. It's often easier to use your imagination with your eyes closed. Allow yourself to feel your body breathing—in and out. Let your body find its natural rhythm.

Take a few moments to allow yourself to imagine a place where you feel safe, comfortable, and relaxed. This can be a real or imagined place, but it should be somewhere that allows you to breathe comfortably and let go of any worry. Perhaps this place is in nature—a beach or an opening in the woods near a brook—or maybe it's a corner of your bedroom or the comfort of a good friend's house. It might even be an imaginary place, like a cloud. Imagine this place in as much detail as you can, including what you hear, smell, and (most of all) feel like in this place.

Soon you'll receive a visitor—a warm and kind friend. This is someone who loves you completely and accepts you exactly for who you are. This can be real person, like a friend of yours, a beloved grandparent, or a favorite teacher, or it can be a character from a book you've read, a pet, or even a superhero from a video game, comic book, or movie. It can also be some being that you create from your imagination. Imagine this being in as much detail as possible, especially how it feels to be in their presence.

Your compassionate friend cares deeply about you and just wants you to be happy. Soon you will be greeting this compassionate friend. You can either go out from your safe place to meet your friend, or you can invite them in. Imagine that you are doing that now. Allow yourself to sit with the person at just the right distance, feeling completely comfortable and safe, completely accepted and loved.

Take a moment to enjoy how you feel in the presence of your compassionate friend.

This person or being is here with you now and can understand exactly what it's like to be you. They know exactly where you are in your life right now and understand precisely what you are struggling with. And this person or being accepts and understands you completely for who you are, perhaps better than anyone else.

This being has something important to say to you, something that is just what you need to hear right now. See if you can listen closely for the words they want to share, words that are comforting and supportive.

And if no words come, that's okay too. Just enjoy being in the presence of your compassionate friend.

And now, maybe you have something to say to this friend. This friend is a very good listener, and completely gets you. Is there anything you'd like to say?

Enjoy your friend's good company for a few last moments, and then wave goodbye to your friend, knowing that you can invite them back whenever you need to. You are now alone in your safe place again. Let yourself savor what just happened, perhaps reflecting on the words you heard.

Before this practice ends, please remember that this compassionate friend is a part of you. The presence you felt and the words you heard are a deep part of yourself. The comfort and safety that you may be feeling is there within you at all times. Know that you can return to this safe place and to this compassionate friend whenever you need to.

Bringing your attention back to your breath, gently open your eyes if they've been closed.

Inquiry

- How was it doing this practice compared to earlier in the program?

- Were you able to find a safe place this time? Did you get a visit from your compassionate friend?

- What was it like remembering that you have that wise and compassionate voice within you?

Self-Appreciation

5 minutes

Intention

- Cultivate self-appreciation
- Recognize how gratitude for others and self-gratitude are connected

Talking Points

- We can be grateful for many things in our lives but are rarely grateful for the positive qualities in ourselves. We tend to criticize ourselves, focus on our inadequacies, and take our good qualities for granted, thereby not really appreciating ourselves. This gives us a skewed perspective of who we are.

- Is there anyone in the room who finds it difficult to receive a compliment?

- Often, when we receive a compliment, it bounces right off us, but when we receive the slightest negative feedback, we fixate on it. It feels uncomfortable to even *think* about what's good about ourselves.

- Why do you think it is so hard to celebrate our good qualities? [*Students may offer up a variety of suggestions, such as "We're taught that praising ourselves is bragging, and that's rude," "We don't want to alienate others by seeming arrogant," or "We may feel guilty or fake."*]

- Often, we're afraid of compliments because it distinguishes us from others and places us ahead of them. This results in a type of disconnection, when what we really need more than anything is to be connected with others. In this way, we don't want to stand out.

- To appreciate your good qualities and fully appreciate yourself, you must remember two key truths:
  - **Common humanity:** Everyone has strengths and good qualities. Acknowledging the fact that you have some good qualities doesn't mean that others don't, or that others have fewer good qualities. We all have strengths. We are all alike in this way.
  - **Interdependence:** Our humanity means that we are all connected to each other. We are who we are, in part, because of the influences we have had on each other.

In South Africa, this is reflected in the concept of *ubuntu*, which translates to "I am because we are." That means that our strengths and good qualities are influenced by multiple factors beyond ourselves. When we can recognize that our strengths are, in part, a product of those who helped us develop them, it helps us feel more connected with them.

What Would I Like to Remember?

15 minutes

Intention

- Put into words the most important lessons from the program, as a reminder for future practice

Instructions

- Read the following script to students:

  Our class is nearly over, and we have learned a lot of principles and practices of mindfulness and self-compassion. In order to reinforce our learning, we are going to write ourselves a private letter about the things we would like to remember from our time together.

  Please take out a pen and use the personalized paper you created at the beginning of class to write a private letter to yourself.

  Before you begin writing, please close your eyes for a moment and take two deep breaths.

  Now ask yourself: "In this class, what touched me, moved me, or shifted something for me?" Perhaps there are particular moments, comments, or insights that really impacted you. [Long pause]

  When you're ready, open your eyes and begin writing a letter to yourself, writing in the same tone you would use when writing to a close friend. Write to yourself sensitively and compassionately! [Long pause]

  Now, ask yourself the question "What worked for me?" Please invite yourself to return to any practices that were interesting, enjoyable, or meaningful to you, and that you might wish to remember and practice in the future. [Long pause]

  When you're ready, begin writing your answer to this question in the same compassionate and supportive voice.

- As the students are writing their answers to the second question, show a slide of the toolkit containing all the practices from all 16 sessions.

  Now write a promise or pledge to yourself of what you will take from this program given what you have learned. For example, "I found out this important thing about me, or I learned this cool practice, so I promise myself to do more of something good (a practice, a kindness, a core value) and less of something that no longer serves me in the same way it once did." What promise or pledge do you want to make to yourself?

Once you have finished writing your letter, sign it affectionately, put it in an envelope, seal it, and address it to yourself. You will seal the envelope because I will not read it. Your letter is entirely private. Please give it to me, and I will mail it to you in a month as a reminder of what we learned together.

Teaching Tip: It is helpful to draw a model of an envelope on the board, describing where on the envelope students should write the delivery address and the return address. Many teens no longer know how to address envelopes (but still love getting mail!). As an alternative to writing a physical letter to themselves, students can send an email to themselves that will be delivered at some time in the future. This can be done through the website www.futureme.org. They can do the same exercise (answering the two questions and writing a pledge) in the context of the email.

Sharing Thoughts

5 minutes

Intention

- Provide a symbolic and meaningful close to the program

Instructions

- If you'd like, have students stand in a circle, shoulder to shoulder (or, alternatively, they can stay at their desks).

- Invite students to share one word or sentence about what the class meant to them. Then have them ring a bell or chime and pass it to the person on their right or left.

- Explain to students how the class has been supported and nourished by the presence of each person in the room and how the learning that took place would not have happened without each person.

- Make sure to also recognize the unseen hands who made it possible for you to meet each week for this purpose, including school administrators, other school staff, possibly parents or caregivers, and so on.

- Although this is the final toolkit (for now), encourage students to add more as they find ways to be kind and supportive to themselves.

Toolkit	
Informal Tools	**Formal Tools**
1. Supportive Gestures	1. Sunbathing
2. Good Friend Question (Ask yourself: How would I treat a friend?)	2. Compassionate Friend
3. Sound Practice	3. Compassionate Body Scan
4. Soles of the Feet	4. Affectionate Breathing
5. Mindful Eating	5. Kindness for Someone You Care About
6. Here-and-Now Stone	6. A Person Just Like Me
7. Three Soothing Breaths	7. Calming Music
8. Finding Kindness Phrases	8. Compassionate Letter Writing
9. Soften, Support, Open	9. Giving and Receiving Compassion
10. Exploring Unmet Needs (Ask yourself: What's beneath the anger?)	10. Noticing Sounds
11. Savoring (Notice things that make you smile and savor them)	11. Gratitude (Write down three things that you're grateful for each day)

CHAPTER 5

Drop-In Sessions

> 66 Anytime I hear the patter of negativity and self-criticism starting to get loud in my brain, when my doubts begin to build, I try to pause for a moment and call it as I see it. I've been practicing stepping back and addressing my fear with familiarity, offering no more than a half-friendly shrug and a few easy words:
>
> Oh, hello. It's you again.
>
> Thanks for showing up. For making me so alert.
>
> But I see you.
>
> You're no monster to me.
>
> **—Michelle Obama**

Over the years, I have heard from many school counselors and teachers who didn't always have the time to deliver the full 16-session curriculum. Often, they only could afford 10 or 15 minutes within the school day to introduce and reinforce self-compassion practices, and scheduling these times wasn't necessarily predictable. It was based on these conversations that I decided to create a series of short "mini" sessions that educators could use when they had limited time on their hands. Some of these lessons were adapted from the semester-long curriculum and need some concept building prior to being taught, while others were specifically created as standalone drop-in sessions. Those that require concept building can be taught successively across two to four sessions and are indicated as such throughout this chapter.

The drop-in sessions in this chapter cover the topics of:

- Mindfulness

- Self-compassion

- Gratitude

- Agency and purpose

Given that mindfulness is foundational to self-compassion—we need to be aware that we're struggling in order to take the essential steps to address and alleviate our struggles—it's best to start with the mindfulness drop-in sessions first. However, you can also return to these mindfulness practices at any point, particularly if students would benefit from lowering their stress and anxiety. For example, you can offer the *Palm of the Hand* or *Soles of the Feet* practices before students take a test.

Mindfulness Practices

The 16-session curriculum contains a number of mindfulness practices that you can introduce at any time, using the previous instructions noted in part 2 of this book. These include:

1. *Sound Practice* (session 3)

2. *Soles of the Feet* (session 3)

3. *Wandering Mind* (session 4)

4. *Here-and-Now Stone* (session 4)*

5. *Mindful Eating* (session 4)**

6. *Calming Music* (session 7)

7. *Opening Art Activities* from sessions 1–9

In addition to these practices, there are several additional practices not included in the 16-session curriculum that can be useful in reinforcing mindfulness, which are outlined on the following pages.

Many of these are mindful movement exercises that help get students out of their heads and make them more aware of their physical sensations, which is particularly helpful given that students often do not move enough during the school day. These exercises are adapted from theater games that actors play to loosen up prior to a performance. Given that students of this age are often self-conscious of their bodies, it can be helpful to reinforce that these exercises are games and to introduce them in a playful manner, using humor and levity. What makes the games "mindful" is that students must pay close attention in order to be successful. As the games capture their attention, there isn't time for their minds to wander.

---

* The topic of the *Wandering Mind* should be taught together with *Here-and-Now Stone*. Remember to include a transition from one to the other, such as "To help you keep your mind in the present, we have a tool—a stone."

** An expanded version of *Mindful Eating* is provided in this chapter.

"Object" Toss

Intention

- Build community and increase a sense of comfort among teens

- Cultivate mindful attention and awareness

Instructions

- To begin, instruct students to stand in a circle. One person begins by tossing an imaginary object to another person across the circle, indicating what the object is. For example, they might say, "Pablo, I'm tossing you a volleyball!" and pretend to toss the "ball" to Pablo.

- Pablo then "catches" the volleyball and instantaneously it "turns into" something else. Pablo indicates this by saying something like "I've got it! And, oh my goodness, it's now a huge wad of chewing gum!" He pantomimes that he has caught the wad of gum, then "tosses" it to someone else, saying "Elsa, it's coming your way!"

- Elsa then pretends she's catching it and indicates what it has turned into by exclaiming, for example, "It's a huge bowling ball!" She might then pretend that she's being weighed down by the bowling ball. In turn, Elsa then "tosses" it to the next person, until everyone has had a turn to catch and toss the object.

- Encourage students to have fun with this game, being creative about what the object "turns into." Objects that tend to be the most fun are those that vary in size and weight, such as feather, balloon, snowball, car, and so on.

Discussion

- Did you notice your mind wandering while playing this game? Why or why not?

- What did you notice as the object was being tossed to you?

- Did you notice any emotions arising as you did this exercise? For example, some people feel nervous that the object is going to be tossed to them and they won't know what to turn it into, while others can't wait for it to be tossed to them. What did you notice?

Pass the Symbol

Intention

- Build community and increase a sense of comfort among students

- Cultivate mindful attention and awareness

Instructions

- Instruct students to stand in a circle, with one student leaving the room or going to a corner of the room and shutting their eyes.

- Then have each student choose a specific symbol that is theirs for the duration of the game. A symbol is a movement that students can do easily and quickly, such as touching their eyebrow, holding up two fingers as a "peace" symbol, winking an eye, or shrugging their shoulders.

- Ask students in the circle to demonstrate their symbol to everyone else. Make sure everyone is paying careful attention because they will need to remember at least two or three symbols to play the game.

- Next, have students silently pick one person in the circle to be the "leader" who starts the game.

- Ask the student who left the circle to return and stand in the center of the circle. The object of the game is for this person to "catch" where the symbol is.

- When the student in the center of the circle isn't looking, the leader makes the symbol of someone else, such as Julio. The goal is to try to "pass the symbol" without the person in the center seeing who "has" it and who it is being passed to.

- Julio then does a third person's symbol. The symbol continues to be "passed" around the circle in this way, while the person inside the circle tries to "catch" who has the symbol.

- When the person in the center finally guesses correctly, someone else can become the guesser, and the game starts over again.

Discussion

- What were you paying attention to while playing this game?

- What did you notice about your quality of attention? For example, did you notice your attention wandering? Why or why not?

- What did you notice about how you were feeling when the symbol was being passed? Some people are nervous, while others are excited.

Who's the Leader?

Intention

- Build community and increase a sense of comfort among teens

- Cultivate mindful attention and awareness

Instructions

- This game starts out like *Pass the Symbol*, with one person leaving the room (or going to a corner of the room with their eyes closed) and the remaining students silently choosing a leader for the game.

- Once students have chosen a leader, the student who was out of the circle returns and stands in the circle. When their back is turned to the leader, the leader begins an action, such as clapping their hands.

- Everyone else in the circle immediately follows the action.

- After a few seconds, the leader switches to another action, such as touching their nose.

- They continue in this manner while the person who is in the center of the circle tries to guess who the leader is.

- When the person in the center finally guesses correctly, someone else can become the guesser, and the game starts over again.

Discussion

- What were you paying attention to while playing this game?

- What did you notice about your quality of attention? For example, did you notice your attention wandering? Why or why not?

- What do you think helped you pay attention?

EXERCISE

Name Game

Intention

- Build community and increase a sense of comfort among teens

- Cultivate mindful attention and awareness

Instructions

- Prior to the game, gather several bean bags or soft, easily catchable stuffed animals to use in the game.

- To begin the game, invite everyone to stand in a circle and give one student a bean bag.

- The student who is holding the bean bag then says their own name, says the name of another group member, and tosses the bean bag to this group member.

- The person who catches the bean bag repeats the same steps (i.e., says their own name and the name of someone else in the circle) until everyone has had a turn catching the bean bag and tossing it to someone else.

- Once one entire cycle has been completed by the whole group, repeat the cycle again in the same order so group members feel comfortable with the process.

- When everyone is comfortable with this pattern, introduce a second bean bag into the cycle and follow the same order as the first bean bag.

- Emphasize that the goal is to not drop the bean bag. But when this happens, which it will, make sure to be encouraging and ask students, "What would help you not drop the bean bags?" A student might say, "Maybe if we kept our eye on the person throwing it to us" or "Everyone should throw it underhanded, not overhanded, so it's easier to catch."

- Incorporate at least one suggestion from the students and proceed with tossing the bean bags in the same pattern.

- Continue this cycle by adding one or two more bean bags at least two times through.

- If time allows, you can expand this game by going backward. Continue in this way until the person who began the toss gets the bean bag.

Discussion

- What were you paying attention to while playing this game?

- What did you notice about your quality of attention? For example, did you notice your attention wandering? Why or why not?

- What are some things that you could do as a group so that the bean bags don't fall to the floor?

Mirroring

Intention

- Practice paying attention on purpose while connecting with others

- Offer the direct experience of mindful movement

Instructions

- Explain to students that they will be doing an exercise in mindful movement involving self-direction and guided direction.

- Have each student pair with a partner and find a place in the room to stand opposite to one another.

- Once everyone is paired up, the pair will decide who will start as the leader and who will start as the "mirror," or follower.

- Instruct students to begin by either closing their eyes, if that's comfortable for them, or simply allowing their gaze to rest on the floor, directing their attention into the soles of their feet. This helps orient their attention to their bodies.

- Then direct the followers to open their eyes while the leaders keep their eyes closed or allow their gaze to gently rest on the floor.

- Now, have the leaders begin moving their body. Their movements might be slow, precise, and reflect what is needed in that moment. For example, the leader might want to stretch, do shoulder rolls, or gentle twists. Encourage nourishing, soothing movements that provide comfort.

- When the leader moves, the follower mirrors the movement, just as a mirror would, reflecting the leader's image.

- After two minutes, students can switch roles with their partner.

Discussion

- What were you paying attention to while playing this game?

- What did you notice about your quality of attention? For example, did you notice your attention wandering? Why or why not?

- Was it easier being the leader or the follower? Why do you think?

Palm of the Hand

Intention

- Anchor attention to a focal object as a way of staying in the present moment

Instructions

- Similar to the *Here-and-Now Stone* practice in session 4, this practice brings students' attention to an object—in this case, the palm of the hand. If you aren't comfortable giving stones to your students, this is a great alternative. To begin, read the following script to students:

Open the palm of your hand. Take some time to have a good look at it, noticing the slightly different shades of skin on your palm. Have you ever noticed that the skin on your palm isn't exactly all one color?

Now look closely at the lines on your palm—the creases. Notice how some creases lead into each other or how some little creases come from the bigger, main creases. Notice the difference in coloration between the main creases, the little creases, and the rest of the palm of your hand.

Experiment with stretching your hand out so your fingers bend back slightly and the skin is stretched taut across your hand. Do you notice any changes in the lines on your hand?

How does it feel when you stretch your hand out like this? What sensations do you notice? What happens when you hold this stretch for a few more seconds? Stretch it out even further. What do you notice now? Any other changes? What happens when you hold the stretch for a minute or more? Do you notice any thoughts coming up in your mind?

Now relax your hand and let the fingers naturally curl slightly inward. How does this change the sensations that you can feel? How does this change what the palm of your hand looks like?

Relax your hand even more and see what happens to your fingers and your palm. Are there any changes in the color or the creases in your hand? And what about in your thoughts? Do you notice any new thoughts arising in your mind?

Now, with one finger of your other hand, gently trace the lines in your palm. Notice the physical sensation that you're feeling. Keep your attention on the contact point where your finger touches the palm of your hand. What does that point of contact feel like?

Next, close your eyes if this is comfortable for you, and make slow circles with your finger around the surface of your palm, keeping your attention on the sensation you are feeling.

When your mind wanders, gently guide your attention back to the sensation of your finger on your palm. You may even want to add more fingers to the mix and notice what the sensation is like when you trace your palm down to the tips of each finger. You can do this for as long as you like. When you're ready, you can gently open your eyes if they were closed.

As you were doing this practice, you may have noticed you weren't worrying and stressing so much. That's because you were staying in the present moment by using your sense of sight and your sense of touch. Physical sensations keep you in the present moment and allow you to let go of the past and future—where worry and stress take place.

Inquiry

- What did you notice about the sensations on your hand?

- Were you able to come back to the sensation in your hand even if your mind wandered? Luckily, you always have your hand with you! You can do this practice whenever you start to feel stressed, and it will bring you back to the present moment.

Compassionate Movement to Wake Up the Body

Intention

- Bring awareness to what the body needs

- Bring energy into the body after sitting for some time

Instructions

- Read the following script to students:

Stand up and feel the soles of your feet on the floor. I then invite you to begin rocking forward and backward, side to side, and notice the changing sensations in the soles of the feet. Anchor your awareness in the feet.

Now, open your field of awareness and notice other sensations in your body, particularly noting any areas of tension or discomfort.

Gradually begin to move your body in a way that feels good to move, perhaps letting yourself gently rock back and forth, rolling your head, twisting at the waist, bending forward or side to side—whatever feels right for you right now.

Letting your body move as it would like to move, noting where it needs to stretch and giving your body the stretch it needs.

When you are ready, come back to standing again and feeling your body.

Now, starting with the top of one shoulder, use the other hand to gently tap down your arm on both sides to "wake it up." Tap down your arm on the outside from the shoulder to your hand, and then up the underside of your arm back to your underarm.

Then do the same with the other arm and hand.

Now, with both hands, tap down one of your legs—all the way to your foot—and then back up your calf and thigh.

Then do the same with the other leg and foot.

Now, use one hand to gently tap your upper chest, the sides and back of your neck, and then your forehead, your cheeks, the area around your nose and eyebrows, and the top and sides of your head.

Rub both hands together until they generate some warmth, then close your eyes and gently place the heels of your hands over your closed eyes. They can be kept there until the warmth has dissipated.

Finally, gently massage the back of your neck, the pressure points near the base of your skull, the area at your temples, your forehead, and any other place around your head that feels like it might benefit from a bit of a massage.

Take a moment to notice how your body feels, particularly any other areas that need to be stretched or attended to in any way before returning to sitting down.

Inquiry

- What changes did you notice before doing the exercise compared to now?

- Did you notice your mind wandering? If so, what did you do?

EXERCISE

What's in My Frame?

Intention

- Bring students' attention and awareness to their physical surroundings

- Help students appreciate aspects of the outdoors that they may not have been aware of before

Instructions

- Give students frames made from cardboard. The frames can be 1–2 inches wide and any size. In general, frames that have a 1×1-foot opening work well. (Alternatively, wire hangers in which the triangle of the hanger is stretched out to a circle can be used.)

- Have the class go outside and instruct each student to find an area and toss the frame in front of them. Wherever the frame lands is their "space."

- Ask students to take their time using their senses to observe what is in their space. For example, if students are in a grassy area, they might notice drops of dew on the blades of grass or the sun glistening on the dew. They can even take a moment to feel the moisture of the dew. Or if students are on an asphalt playground, they may notice the glinting of the sun as it reflects off the different types of rock in the asphalt, and they may spend a minute or two noticing the roughness of the asphalt.

- If, after a few minutes, students say, "I've seen everything, now what do I do?" gently encourage them to take another look. Convey to them that there is always more to see.

- After 10 minutes (this will vary depending on the age and maturity of students), return to the classroom and, if time allows, discuss their experience.

Discussion

- What did you notice when you were looking at your square? The space within your frame?

- Did you see anything that surprised you?

- When you thought you were finished and I told you to look again, what did you discover?

206

Mindful Eating (Expanded)

Intention

- Cultivate an awareness that our senses are a portal to the present moment

Instructions

- After you have introduced mindful eating with a dried cranberry (or another fruit) in session 4, it can be interesting to explore what other foods taste like when eaten mindfully. Some may be very surprising! Use the drop-in sessions as an opportunity to introduce different foods using the previous script from session 4. For example, one session can involve mindfully eating a potato chip, and the next session can focus on a small piece of fruit, like a strawberry, grape, or slice of orange.

- In general, foods that are highly processed and include many additives (such as potato chips) don't taste nearly as good as people think they do when eaten mindfully. Processed foods are designed to be eaten quickly without taking time to take in their full flavor. On the other hand, a well-ripened piece of fruit is replete with flavor and texture, and students may be impressed with how flavorful it is.

- When leading this exercise, it's important for students to come up with their own conclusions based on their own observations. If they decide that cheese-flavored tortilla chips are "the bomb" when eaten mindfully and raisins still taste awful, so be it. This exercise is not about getting students to eat more healthful foods—or getting them to eat in any particular way for that matter. It is simply about giving them an opportunity to see things as they are without any kind of preconceived ideas.

- Remember that mindfulness is simply about noticing the present moment without any layer of interpretation (such as "I know potato chips are awesome because I've had them before—therefore, I know this potato chip is awesome"). Allow students the opportunity to explore each food as if they've never experienced it before. Let them try it for themselves slowly and mindfully, using all their senses, and allow them to come to their own conclusions.

- Let the students lead the way. This is their learning process. You are simply a guide—a witness even—to this process. Your job is to ask the right questions to help them see clearly what's already in front of them.

Advanced Mindful Eaters Variation

- Once students become experienced trying different foods and eating them mindfully, you can introduce foods that might generate more of a reaction, such as a small piece of candy (e.g., jellybeans), chocolate, a brussels sprout, or a piece of a sardine.

- Be aware, however, that the objective of this advanced lesson would be somewhat different. It wouldn't simply be about noticing physical sensations but also about noticing thoughts arising in the mind and emotional reactions to the food (the "yum" or "yuck" response). You want students to notice how their bodies feel when they sense aversion versus when they anticipate eating something delicious.

- You can follow the *Mindful Eating* instructions in session 4 to help guide the process and use the additional discussion questions here to address students' emotional reactions to the food. It's best to ask these questions when the reactions first surface in the class.

Discussion

- I'm noticing some reactions from many of you about these _____ (e.g., jellybeans). What are you feeling right now? [*You can pass out an image of the* Emotion Wheel *(in appendix 2) to help facilitate discussion of emotions.*]

- How would you describe your emotion?

- If you pay attention to your body, do you notice anything happening? For example, do you notice your heart beating faster? Do you notice if you are salivating?

- Have you noticed any changes in your ability to pay attention now compared to before I brought out this food?

Thoughts Are Not Facts

Intention

- Provide an introduction to the *Thoughts Are Not Facts* exercise

- Set the groundwork for students to begin to question their thoughts, particularly those that lead to negative conclusions

Background

One of the most interesting lessons that mindfulness teaches us is that our thoughts are not facts. We are very used to not questioning our thoughts—to see them as solid and undeniable truths. After all, they feel so real! This was illustrated to me clearly some years ago when my then 20-year-old daughter called me crying, saying "Grandpa hates me!" When I asked her why she thought this, she explained, "I called him, he answered the phone, and when he heard my voice, he hung up!" I immediately knew what had happened. Her grandfather—my father—was extremely hard of hearing, and I'm sure he didn't hear her voice on the other end of the phone. He thought no one was there, so he hung up. Yet my daughter had created a narrative to understand why her grandfather had hung up the phone, and that narrative included the fact that her grandfather hated her, which of course I knew was not true.

When we realize that our thoughts are simply random ideas that our minds come up with to make sense of what is going on in our lives, we experience a perceptible shift in how we see ourselves and our relationship with ourselves. We take ourselves less seriously, and with it, our previously tightly held negative beliefs about ourselves start to loosen and eventually unravel. Understanding that "our thoughts are not facts" can be eye-opening for students.

Talking Points

- Our minds are constantly generating thoughts to help us understand the events in our lives. Usually, these thoughts are far worse than the truth of why the event happened. For example, if someone is upset because they were not invited to an event involving a group of friends, their mind may generate thoughts such as:

  - "They don't like me."

- o "I'm not worthy."

- o "I'm stupid."

- o "I'm not cool."

- o "No one wants to be seen with me."

- One reason that our minds generate these negative thoughts is because it wants to prepare us for the worst so that we're not caught off guard the next time something like this happens. In other words, if we convince ourselves that we weren't invited because people don't like us, then maybe we won't be as hurt if this occurs again at a later time. We'll be mentally prepared.

- When we slow down, as mindfulness teaches us to do, we can recognize that the thoughts in our minds are just that—thoughts. They're just ideas that bubble up out of our brains and are not necessarily true at all. Naturally, they feel very real to us, but that doesn't make them true. As someone once said, "Don't believe everything you think!" When we are able to remember that, we are free from being attached to these thoughts.

- Whenever you get caught up in the "stories" that your mind tells you, remember that you may not have all the information you need to come to any kind of conclusion. The best thing to do is wait and gather more info.

Thoughts Are Not Facts

Intention

- Provide a clear way for students to have the opportunity to realize that simply thinking a thought does not mean that it is actually true

Instructions

- Read the following script to students:

If you're comfortable closing your eyes, then go ahead and do that. Sometimes it's easier to use your imagination with your eyes closed. It's also fine to keep them partly open.

Now, imagine that you're walking down the hallway at school at the end of the day. Visualize the scene—maybe lockers are slamming shut, lots of kids are milling around, and teachers are chatting with students. At the end of the hallway, you see a group of kids, some of whom you know, and you start to walk toward them. Before you reach them, you see one of them glance your way, and they all start to laugh.

What thoughts are going through your mind at this moment? What feelings come up for you? What physical sensations do you notice? Take a few minutes to write down your thoughts, feelings, and physical sensations.

What is your explanation of what happened? Of why the group started to laugh? Please write this down also and be honest. No one will read this—it is only for you.

Now, close your eyes again and imagine the same scene. Again, you're walking down the hall and see the same group of people, some of whom you know. You start to walk toward them. One of them glances your way, and they all start to laugh. The person who glanced toward you rushes over to you and says, "Oh my goodness, I have to tell you the most hilarious thing that Andros just told us about what happened in math class!"

Now what are your thoughts? Feelings? Physical sensations? How are your responses different in the two scenarios?

Can you see how we all make assumptions to help us understand situations when we don't have all the information?

This is a reminder that our thoughts are not necessarily always true. Our mind creates these stories as an attempt to explain what took place. Often, these stories are worse than the truth because, in a way, our mind is trying to prepare us for the worst. So it's important to not take our thoughts too seriously.

- After you have completed the exercise, one way to help students remind themselves to not take their thoughts as truths is to guide them through the following steps:

  o When students find themselves thinking a negative thought, such as "I know they're laughing at me," they can ask themselves the question "Am I sure?"

  o Then see what comes up for them. Can they be sure? If their immediate response is "Oh yeah, I'm sure!" then encourage them to dig deeper and ask, "Am I *really* sure?" If their response is still yes, then encourage them to ask, "Am I really, *really* sure?" and then, if needed, "Am I really, really, *100 percent* sure?"

  o Most of the time, students will find that they really can't be 100 percent sure about many things in their lives.

Inquiry

- What stands out to you about this activity?

- What did you discover from doing it that you might not have known before?

Self-Compassion Practices

The following self-compassion practices, exercises, and topics can be offered at any time using the instructions provided in the 16-session curriculum. They do not need previous sessions on mindfulness or self-compassion.

1. *Sunbathing* (session 1)

2. *Supportive Gestures* (session 2)

3. *Compassionate Body Scan* (session 4)

4. *Affectionate Breathing* (session 5)

5. *Three Soothing Breaths* (session 5)

6. *Kindness for Someone You Care About* (session 6)

7. *Practicing with Kindness Phrases* (session 6)

8. *Finding Kindness Phrases* (session 6)*

9. *A Person Just Like Me* (session 7)**

10. *Self-Compassion* (session 8)

11. *Japanese Bowls* (session 10)

12. *The Adolescent Brain* (session 14)

13. *Gratitude* (session 15)

14. *Finding Gratitude* (session 15)

In contrast, the following practices need to be taught at a particular time because students need a foundational understanding of self-compassion and experience in using self-compassion tools. The practices that are listed together should be taught concurrently or in consecutive sessions, with adequate review of the topic discussed in the first session provided in the second session.

1. *Compassionate Friend* (session 1): This is a terrific guided practice to introduce early on because it helps students realize that they have a compassionate voice within themselves that they can call upon when needed. However, at times, students may envision someone they loved who has passed away, and this can be emotionally challenging for them.

   When introducing this practice in the classroom, make sure that you have time for discussion following the practice so that students have the opportunity to process any challenging feelings if they choose to do so. Remember that becoming emotionally challenged during this program is not

---

* You can offer *Kindness for Someone You Care About* in one session, with *Practicing with Kindness Phrases* and *Finding Kindness Phrases* offered in consecutive sessions.

** An expanded version of *A Person Just Like Me* is offered in this chapter.

necessarily a bad thing, as you are teaching students how to manage difficult emotions. However, you need to make sure that enough time is provided to resolve these feelings.

If you are working with a group that has experienced significant trauma, or you feel that some students might have difficulty imagining a compassionate friend, you can begin slowly by presenting this practice in three parts—(1) creating a safe place, (2) meeting your compassionate friend, and (3) receiving a gift. This three-part version is offered in subsequent pages. Note that the version of *Compassionate Friend* included in the 16-session curriculum does not include "receiving a gift" because it is a lot of content for students to digest in one session.

2. *How Would I Treat a Friend?* (session 2): Since this exercise is eye-opening to teens and helps them understand why we practice self-compassion, it's important to introduce this early on—in the first or second session, for example.

3. *Self-Criticism and Safety/Motivating Ourselves with Compassion* (session 8): This exercise can be emotionally activating to students once they realize that they have spent much of their lives unnecessarily beating themselves up in response to their inner critic. For this reason, students need to have a basic understanding of what self-compassion is and be familiar with self-compassion tools prior to introducing this topic and exercise. *Supportive Gestures* and *Finding Kindness Phrases* are two different self-compassion tools that you can introduce prior to this exercise, as well as any mindfulness tools.

4. *Self-Esteem vs. Self-Compassion* (session 9): Students need a basic understanding of what self-compassion is in order to understand the difference between self-compassion and self-esteem. Therefore, it is important to first introduce the definition of self-compassion—either the informal definition (treating yourself as you would treat a good friend who is struggling) or the formal definition (mindfulness, common humanity, and self-kindness)—before leading this exercise.

5. *The Cost of Social Comparison* (session 9): As this exercise asks students to use self-compassion tools, it should be introduced at some point after familiarizing students with tools like *Supportive Gestures*, *Finding Kindness Phrases*, or *Affectionate Breathing*.

6. *Crossing the Line* (session 10): Similar to the *Motivating Ourselves with Compassion* exercise, this exercise should be taught after several self-compassion tools have been introduced, as students may need to provide themselves with reassurance and comfort when they realize that so many others struggle as they do.

7. *Giving and Receiving Compassion* (session 12): Since this guided practice is grounded within the practice of *Affectionate Breathing*, it should be taught well after students are familiar with this breathing practice and have a solid understanding of what compassion "feels" like.

8. *Finding Value in Our Struggles/Silver Linings* (session 12): These lessons should be taught together and only after several self-compassion tools are introduced since the *Silver Linings* exercise asks students to recall past difficult situations that were emotionally challenging. It is important for students to have ways to support and comfort themselves as needed after this exercise.

9. *Working with Difficult Emotions/Soften, Support, Open* (session 13): These lessons are best taught together since the topic provides the conceptual foundation for the practice. They can be taught consecutively on separate days, as long as the concepts from the first lesson are reviewed in the second lesson. Because difficult emotions are just that—difficult—these lessons should be taught after students have a solid foundation in self-compassion.

10. *Working with Anger/Exploring Unmet Needs* (session 14): Similarly, these two lessons should either be taught together or consecutively, as the topic provides the conceptual foundation for the practice. They can be taught consecutively on separate days, as long as the concepts from the first lesson are reviewed in the second lesson. Given that students should only explore their unmet needs once they know how to compassionately meet these needs, introduce these lessons only after students have learned some self-compassion tools.

A Person Just Like Me
(Expanded)

Intention

- Demonstrate common humanity

- Demonstrate compassion for others

Instructions

- In addition to introducing this practice as it is written in session 7, you can expand upon it in several ways. For example, rather than asking students to think of a "random" person in class, you can suggest that they visualize a good friend as you lead them through the practice. At another time, you can lead them through the practice and suggest they think of a teacher in the school.

- If you think that students are ready, you can also suggest that they think of someone they find a bit annoying or who rubs them the wrong way. Because we're generally not comfortable extending good wishes to someone we don't like, this can be somewhat challenging. However, it can also have interesting outcomes. Students may realize that this difficult person in their life also struggles, which is something that may not have occurred to them before.

Inquiry

- What came up for you when you did this practice for a good friend (or teacher, or annoying person)?

- What thoughts or feelings did you notice? Did anything surprise you?

- How might this change the way you behave toward this person?

Compassionate Friend in Three Parts

Part 1: Compassionate Friend—Finding a Safe Space

Intention

- Help students find an imaginary safe place they can return to when needed

Instructions

- Read the following script to students:

If you'd like to fold your arms and put your head down on your desk, feel free to do that. Allow your eyes to close, if that feels okay to you, and begin by taking a few deep breaths, allowing your shoulders to relax.

Take a few moments to allow yourself to imagine a place where you feel safe, comfortable, and relaxed. This can be a real or imagined place, but it should be somewhere that allows you to breathe comfortably and let go of any worry. Perhaps this place is in nature—a beach or an opening in the woods near a brook—or maybe it's a corner of your bedroom or the comfort of a good friend's house. It might even be an imaginary place, like a cloud.

You're allowed to bring any objects that you would like to this space. Is there something particularly special and meaningful that you would like to bring in? Perhaps a book or two, a stuffed animal, a favorite blanket or T-shirt, maybe even a pet? You're encouraged to bring in anything that helps you feel comforted and safe.

Is there any music or sounds you'd like to have in this space? You can keep it silent if you'd like, have sounds of nature, or bring in music. The only requirement is that this music is soothing and comforting to you.

What are you sitting on in this space? Is it a big comfy chair, a couch, a bed? Or maybe you're sprawled out on the floor with some giant pillows. If you're in nature, maybe you're lying on your back on the forest floor, or on the sand at a beach, or somewhere else.

Imagine this place in as much detail as you can, including what you hear, smell, and (most of all) feel like in this place.

Let yourself enjoy the feeling of being here in this space. Savor this moment, letting it soak in. Know that however you feel right now is just how you feel. There's no right or wrong way to feel. Whatever you feel is how you're meant to feel.

In a minute or two, you'll be leaving this safe place. Before you do, make sure to look around and take it all in. You can return to this safe space whenever you like. It is always here for you.

Whenever you feel ready, you can leave this space. If your eyes have been closed, you can gently open your eyes.

Inquiry

- Were you able to find a safe space? If so, what was it like to be in this space?

- What does it feel like knowing you can return to your safe space whenever you'd like?

Part 2: Compassionate Friend—
Meeting Your Compassionate Friend

Intention

- "Meet" the kind voice present within ourselves

Instructions

- Read the following script to students:

If you'd like to fold your arms and put your head down on your desk, feel free to do that. If it feels okay to you, you can close your eyes. If not, just simply keep a downward gaze so you're not distracted by things around you.

Take a few deep breaths, letting go a little bit more each time you breathe out. As you breathe in, you're breathing in the energy you need, and as you breathe out, you're letting go of any stress in your body.

Check in with your shoulders, making sure they're relaxed and away from your ears. Then check in with your mouth and jaw, making sure they're not clenched. And finally, check in with your belly to make sure it is relaxed.

Now, bring to mind your safe place. Maybe this is a place in nature, in your home or a friend's home, or somewhere else entirely. Perhaps it's an imaginary place. Remember you can bring in whatever objects you'd like to make it feel as comfortable and safe as possible. You can make it however you'd like.

Notice how you feel in this space—safe, comfortable—perhaps for the first time ever. Enjoy the feeling of being in this space.

Soon you'll receive a visitor—a warm and kind friend. This is someone who loves you completely and accepts you exactly for who you are. This can be a real person, like a friend of yours, a beloved grandparent, or a favorite teacher, or it can be a character from a book you've read, a pet, or even a superhero from a video game, comic book, or movie. It can also be some being you create from your imagination. Imagine this being in as much detail as possible, especially how it feels to be in their presence.

Your compassionate friend cares deeply about you and just wants you to be happy. Soon you will be greeting this compassionate friend. You can either go out from your safe place to meet your friend, or you can invite them in. Imagine that you are doing that now. Allow yourself to sit with the person at just the right distance, feeling completely comfortable and safe, completely accepted and loved.

Take a moment to enjoy how you feel in the presence of your compassionate friend. This person or being is here with you now and can understand exactly what it's like to be you. They know exactly where you are in your life right now and understand precisely what you are struggling with. And this person or being accepts and understands you completely for who you are, perhaps better than anyone else.

This being has something important to say to you, something that is just what you need to hear right now. See if you can listen closely for the words they want to share, words that are comforting and supportive.

And if no words come, that's okay too. Just enjoy being in the presence of your compassionate friend.

And now, maybe you have something to say to this friend. This friend is a very good listener, and completely understands you. Is there anything you'd like to say?

Enjoy your friend's good company for a few last moments, and then wave goodbye to your friend, knowing that you can invite them back whenever you need to.

You are now alone in your safe place again. Let yourself savor what just happened, perhaps reflecting on the words you heard.

Before this practice ends, please remember that this compassionate friend is a part of you. The presence you felt and the words you heard are a deep part of yourself. The comfort and safety that you may be feeling is there within you at all times. Know that you can return to this safe place and to this compassionate friend whenever you need to.

Whenever you are ready, taking whatever time you need, you can gently open your eyes if they've been closed.

Inquiry

- Did you get a visit from a compassionate friend? If so, what was that like? If you didn't, what was that like?

- Did you get any words from your compassionate friend? What was it like to hear those words? How did it make you feel?

- If you didn't hear any words, what was that like?

Teaching Tip: If students are disappointed because they didn't get a visit from a compassionate friend or didn't hear words from this friend, remind them that sometimes this takes time and encourage them to be patient. It's also perfectly okay if this particular guided practice doesn't work for them. Remind them that there is an array of different practices and tools they can pick and choose from. They don't have to practice all of them!

Part 3: Compassionate Friend— Getting a Gift

Intention

- Recognize that we all have a kind and caring voice within ourselves that is accessible to us at all times

Instructions

- Read the following script to students:

  If you'd like to fold your arms and put your head down on your desk, feel free to do so.

  Now, take a few breaths and allow yourself to relax and settle in. Each time you breathe out, you can let go of a little more stress that's in your body and let yourself sink a little bit deeper into your chair.

  Check in with your shoulders, making sure they're relaxed and away from your ears. Then check in with your mouth and jaw, making sure they're not clenched. And finally, check in with your belly to make sure it is relaxed.

  Now, bring to mind your safe place. Visualize it with all its details, including the objects you've brought in to make it just right for you, the music, and most of all, what it feels like to be in this space.

  Let yourself enjoy being here. Allow yourself to be absorbed by the feeling of warmth and safety that you feel in this place. This is a place that is all yours, where you feel completely protected from anything that could harm you.

  Soon your compassionate friend will arrive to this place. This being knows you better than anyone else and completely loves you and accepts you exactly for who you are. You can either go out to greet your friend or invite them in, whichever feels right to you.

  You are now sitting with your compassionate friend, sitting at just the right distance apart, and your friend is looking at you with the kindest eyes.

  Your friend knows you by heart—knows your wishes and your dreams—and is here to support you. Always. They want you to be happy, and they always have your back.

  Your friend has something to give to you, something that is meaningful to you. This is something that you can take with you, something that will help you remember that this friend is always with you, always looking out for you.

  You hold out your hand, and maybe the object just appears in your hand. Or maybe your compassionate friend reaches over and gives it to you.

You look down, and there it is in your hand. You take a good look and smile because you know what this object means to you.

Soon it will be time for your friend to leave.

Enjoy your friend's good company for a few last moments, and wave goodbye to your friend, knowing that you can invite them back whenever you need to. You are now alone in your safe place again. Let yourself savor what just happened, perhaps reflecting on the gift you were given.

Before this practice ends, please remember that this compassionate friend is a part of you. The presence you felt and the gift you received are a deep part of yourself. The comfort and safety that you may be feeling is there within you at all times. Know that you can return to this safe place and to this compassionate friend whenever you need to.

Whenever you are ready, taking whatever time you need, gently open your eyes if they've been closed.

Inquiry

- How was it to revisit your safe place?

- If you received a gift, what was that like?

- How did it feel to realize that you always have that kind voice within you at all times and that you can go to your safe place and visit your compassionate friend whenever you want to?

A Moment for Me

Intention

- Provide a quick and efficient self-compassion practice that can be applied throughout the day whenever difficult emotions arise

Instructions

- This practice can be taught anytime after you have introduced the formal definition of self-compassion, which includes the explanation of the three components—mindfulness, common humanity, and self-kindness.

- To begin, read the following script to students:

Think of a situation in your life that is difficult or causing you stress. Please choose a situation that is not the worst or most difficult in your life, but one that is causing you some discomfort.

When you think of this situation, can you feel the experience in your body? Perhaps you feel the discomfort as tightness in the chest or a gripping in the stomach?

Now, say to yourself: "In this moment, a part of me is struggling." This is mindfulness. You are identifying how you feel in this moment. You might choose to say to yourself, "Whoa, this feels awful," "This sucks," or maybe "This is stress."

Now, say to yourself: "This kind of struggle is a part of life." This is common humanity. Lots of other people struggle in this same way. You might choose to say, "Other kids feel this way too," "I'm not alone with this feeling," or "This is a part of being a teen, and so many other kids struggle just like me."

Now, offer yourself a kind, soothing, and supportive touch—maybe a hand on your heart or another gesture that feels right for you. Feel the warmth of your hand coming through to your body.

Now, say to yourself: "May I be kind to myself." Remember that as a teen, you're going through so many transitions. Your brain is changing, your body is changing, and you may be in a new school or thinking about college. There are so many pressures and so many changes. So be gentle with yourself.

As you think about the situation you are struggling with, ask yourself: "What do I need to hear right now?" If you have trouble finding the words to say, ask yourself what you would say to a good friend who was going through this. Can you say those words to yourself? For example, you might say:

- *I wish to give myself the compassion that I need.*
- *I wish to accept myself as I am.*

- *I wish to learn to accept myself as I am.*
- *I wish to forgive myself.*
- *I wish to be strong.*
- *I wish to be safe.*
- *I wish to be peaceful.*
- *I wish to know that I deserve love.*

You can also just say words or phrases like "strong" or "accept myself."

Inquiry

- Did anything change when you put your hand on your heart or offered yourself another soothing gesture?

- What is it like to think that you can actually begin to notice when you're struggling and begin to offer yourself kind words?

- What is it like to know that you can actually treat yourself with more kindness?

- Can you think of a situation where this would be useful to you?

Affectionate Breathing
(Expanded)

Intention

- Bring attention to the breath as a mindfulness practice

- Cultivate self-compassion by breathing in what is needed and letting go of what isn't

- Relax and calm the body

Instructions

- After you have introduced *Affectionate Breathing* in session 5, you can offer students this variation, which extends the out-breath and makes it a little bit longer than the in-breath. The reason for doing it this way is that it activates the parasympathetic nervous system, which is the part of the nervous system that relaxes us.

- To begin, read the following script to students:

To begin, please sit comfortably in your chair. Sit upright, imagining there is a string that extends from the crown of your head up to the ceiling. Make sure your shoulders are relaxed and not hunched. This position will support you in being alert and aware. If you're comfortable closing your eyes, please close them. If you'd rather have your eyes open, you can keep your gaze downward so you're not distracted by things around you.

Take a few slow, easy breaths, noticing the breath where it is most obvious to you. Maybe it's the tip of your nose where you're breathing in, the rising and lowering of your chest with each breath, or the area around your diaphragm below your rib cage. Wherever you notice it most easily.

Just feel the breath, from the beginning of the in-breath all the way to the end of the out-breath.

As you breathe in, imagine you are breathing in something that you need, like strength, courage, patience, or tenderness. Perhaps you picture this as a word, an image, or even a color. Whatever works for you. As you breathe in, slowly count to four.

Now, as you breathe out, imagine you are letting go of whatever it is that you are holding on to that you no longer need. Maybe this is tension, discomfort, sadness, a feeling of unworthiness, or anxiety. As you breathe out, slowly count to six. As you breathe out, you might want to imagine this thing that you no longer need leaving your body, going out into space, and dissolving and disappearing.

Continue in this way, breathing in whatever it is that you need for four slow counts, and breathing out whatever you're ready to let go of for six counts.

Whenever the mind wanders, which it will because that's what minds do, gently bring your attention back to the breath. Remember that mind wandering doesn't mean you're doing anything wrong—it's simply the way our minds work.

Breathing in and breathing out.

Keeping this easy, simply breathing in and out.

And whenever you feel ready, you can gently open your eyes.

Inquiry

- What was it like to breathe in something that you needed? What did you notice?

- How did it feel to let go of something that you don't need? What was that like?

- Did you notice anything shift when you made your out-breath a little longer than your in-breath?

Self-Kindness

Intention

- Foster feelings of self-kindness

- Help teens who have trouble offering kindness to themselves first imagine receiving kindness from a loved one

- Deepen the *Kindness for Someone You Care About* practice by using personalized phrases

Instructions

- This practice below should be taught after the kindness series in session 6, as one intention of this practice is to deepen *Kindness for Someone You Care About*.

- To begin, read the following script to students:

Last session, I invited you to find some kindness phrases that resonate with you. Words that you would like to hear every day if you could. If you aren't totally satisfied with the ones you came up with last time, don't worry—you have lots of time to explore phrases that are just right for you! This is only the beginning of the process. Today, I will offer you a few phrases that you are free to use when the time comes. If you have found phrases that you like and want to try them out, feel free to use them here.

Begin by getting into a comfortable position, either sitting on a cushion, couch, or chair or lying down. Fully or partially close your eyes if this is comfortable for you, and take a few deep breaths to settle into your body and into the present moment.

Now, bring to mind someone who is loving, caring, and supportive. It could be your compassionate friend, a grandparent, a pet, a movie character, or someone you create in your own mind. Whatever works for you.

Letting yourself feel what it's like to be in this being's presence, create a vivid image of this being in your mind and allow yourself to enjoy their good company.

Recognize how much this being cares about you and wishes you to be happy and free from struggles, just like every other living being. Imagine them saying to you the words you need to hear, using the kindness phrases that you have chosen.

If you haven't found phrases that are comfortable for you yet, you can use the following phrases:

    ○   *I wish for you to know your own strength.*

    ○   *I wish for you to feel loved.*

    ○   *I wish for you to begin to accept yourself, just as you are.*

[Repeat twice, slowly, then pause.]

Whenever you notice that your mind has wandered, return to these words and the image of this being who cares about you, savoring any warm feelings that may arise and taking your time.

Now, letting go of the image of the other being, allow the full focus of your attention to rest directly on yourself. If you would like, put a hand over your heart and feel the warmth and gentle pressure of your hand. Visualize your whole body in your mind, noticing any stress or uneasiness that may be lingering within you.

Then begin to offer yourself some words of kindness, using your own phrases or these:

    ○   *I wish to know my own strength.*

    ○   *I wish to feel loved.*

    ○   *I wish to begin to accept myself, just as I am.*

[Repeat twice, slowly, then pause.]

Finally, take a few breaths and rest quietly in your own body, accepting whatever your experience is, exactly as it is. You may be feeling warm wishes and compassion, or you may not. Either way is okay. We are simply setting an intention to open your heart and then seeing what happens.

Whenever you are ready, taking whatever time you need, you can gently open your eyes if they've been closed.

Inquiry

- What was it like to hear warm wishes from this compassionate being?

- What happened when you let go of the other being and offered kindness to yourself?

- If you decided to use your own phrases, did it change the experience at all?

<u>EXERCISE</u>

Drawing Your Inner Critic and Compassionate Friend

Intention

- Get a clear visual image of the inner critic and the compassionate friend

- Provide a fun way to engage students with the concept of the inner critic and the compassionate friend

Instructions

- Introduce this exercise after *Motivating Ourselves with Compassion*, which can be found in session 8.

- To begin, tell students that they will be creating two images—one of their inner critic and one of their compassionate friend.

- Although students can use any art materials available, colored pencils are advisable as they permit gradation, whereas markers do not.

- To get them to clarify their image, you might ask:

    o How do you picture these two voices in your mind?

    o What do they wear?

    o What are the expressions like on their faces?

    o What is their posture like?

    o How do they wear their hair?

    o Does either one have a job? If so, what would that be?

    o How do they spend their free time?

    o If you were to give each a name, what would that be?

- Alternatively, you can introduce this activity in two separate sessions, with one focusing on drawing the inner critic and the other focusing on the compassionate friend.

Discussion

- What did you notice about your drawings of your inner critic and your compassionate friend?

- Were you surprised by anything that came up for you?

- If your inner critic looks particularly harsh, can you give yourself support and kindness simply because you have to work with this difficult character?

Gratitude Practices

Over the last couple of years, I have made it a habit to take a moment to notice what's good in my life. Mostly these are simple things, like the absolute pleasure of my morning latte, the enjoyment I get out of playing word games, the so-called weeds in my yard that burst forth with tiny purple and yellow flowers in early spring, the warmth of the sun on my face, the delight of a clean kitchen, or the softness of the bathroom rug under my feet. I also find joy in my dog's ridiculous expression when she wants a treat, the way my cat rubs against my ankles, and the elegant egrets that make their home in the marsh behind my home. I could go on and on.

When we make it a habit to notice, savor, and appreciate these moments—when we orient our attention outward to what's good, rather than dwelling on ourselves and our struggles—our base level of happiness gets a huge boost. In fact, research has shown that gratitude not only has profound effects on our overall mental health but on our physical health as well (Froh et al., 2009; Fritz et al., 2019; Wong et al., 2018). It's really pretty amazing how well this works! The important thing is getting into the regular habit of taking note of the good in life.

In this section are a few tried-and-true gratitude practices. There are loads more you can find on the internet by doing a Google search. Either way, you'll want to introduce these activities to students after going over the topic of gratitude in session 15.

Three Good Things*

Intention

- Bring attention to those things in daily life that bring joy

- Elicit positive emotions, such as contentment, gratefulness, and a sense of awe

- Strengthen the class or school community by doing the challenge together as a group

Instructions

- This exercise is a low-tech way of getting into the habit of gratitude. It serves as a reminder that we do, in fact, have good things going on in our lives all the time—they are simply overrun by negative things, which we tend to remember more clearly. As Barbara Fredrickson, a researcher and scholar at the University of North Carolina at Chapel Hill, has said, "The negative screams at you, but the positive only whispers" (personal communication, July 7, 2023).

- Simply ask students to identify three good things that happened to them that day. These do not have to be what would normally be considered "big" things. It might be easier for them to think of small things, such as listening to a favorite song, making a basketball goal, or wearing a well-loved old T-shirt. Have them write these things down and describe how they felt when these things occurred. For example, they can write, "When I petted the cat, it made me feel calm."

- There is also an app version of this practice for students who prefer to track the practice digitally. It's called, unsurprisingly, Three Good Things. It's super simple—students just select a time when they want to be alerted each day, and when the alert goes off, they type in what they're grateful for and how it made them feel. That's it! Students have the option of sharing it with others or not.

---

* From "Forty-Five Good Things," by J. Brian Sexton and Kathryn C. Adair, 2019, *BMJ Open*, *9*(3), (https://doi.org/10.1136/bmjopen-2018-022695).

- This exercise can even be done as an all-school practice over the public address system each morning. Once students are familiar with the instructions, it takes a grand total of three minutes max to do it, and it's a fun and meaningful activity for everyone in the school to do together—students, teachers, office staff, cafeteria workers, janitors, even parents who are present in the school building. It is great for school spirit and community building!

Discussion

- How do you feel after doing this exercise? For example, do you feel "lighter" than you did before we started?

- Were you able to think of the little things in your life that you're happy about?

Gratitude Letter

Intention

- Articulate feelings of gratitude

- Increase positive mood and overall emotional well-being

Instructions

- Instruct students to think about someone for whom they are grateful. This does not have to be someone who has had a huge effect on their life, but someone who has shown them care and support in even a minor way. For example, it might be a friend who shared some of their lunch with them, a cafeteria worker who smiled at them when serving their food, a teacher who gave them some extra help, or someone in a local store who said a few kind words to them.

- Then ask students to draft a gratitude letter that expresses thanks to the person for what they did. In their letter, make sure students describe how the other person made them feel. They may also want to include how the person's actions may change their own actions toward others in the future.

- Most importantly, the letters need to be authentic expressions from the heart.

- Students do not have to deliver their gratitude letter, as the benefits of gratitude arise from the simple act of expressing gratitude. However, if they would like, they can deliver the letter to the person. This would enhance the effect!

Option for Extending This Exercise

- Incorporate this exercise into a formal writing project (for an English class, for example). Make sure to allow students to get their ideas down first, without worrying about the mechanics of writing, such as grammar, punctuation, or sentence structure. If students are focused on getting their writing correct, the content—the expression of gratitude—will be lost. It is important to encourage them to express their heartfelt feelings of gratitude first, and once that has been completed, they can address the writing mechanics.

Discussion

- How do you feel after writing the letter as compared to how you felt before?

- Is this something that you might want to do again in the future?

Sense-and-Savor Stroll

Intention

- Bring attention to moments all around us that can bring joy

- Increase positive mood

Instructions

- The activity below is a great one to do if you're able to take students outdoors. If that's not possible, it can also be done as a walk around the school or by staying in the classroom. It can be done in 10 to 15 minutes but can also be extended to 30 minutes or longer.

- If you're outdoors, tell students that they will be going on a sense-and-savor stroll. They will have time to wander around the playground (or another area), keeping an eye out for things that draw their attention and bring them a "moment of joy."

- When something draws them in, they can stroll over to it and spend some time using all their senses to take it in. For example, they might notice a leaf or the bark of a tree. They can use their sense of sight to examine the veins in the leaf, its various shades of color, and the way the light might be hitting it. They can use their sense of touch to notice how its texture feels in their hand, their sense of smell to see if it has an odor, or their sense of hearing to see what happens as they run a finger across it. The objective is for them to really enjoy the object that drew them in.

- Once they have spent some time with their object of choice, they can continue their stroll until they find the next object that catches their attention, perhaps ants crawling on the pavement. Students continue this process of using their senses to spend some time enjoying—savoring—each object.

Indoor Stroll Variation

- In this variation, have your class wander slowly together throughout the school.

- Ask each student to keep an eye out for things in the environment that make them smile. This could be anything—a younger student in the hallway, sounds of singing from the music room, or artwork on the hallway wall.

- Whenever they see something, have them write it down in a notepad and describe how it made them feel. For example: "Two little kindergartners were sharing a picture book in the library. I thought it was cute, and it made me happy." Another example might be "A little kid made a basket in the gym while playing basketball, and he jumped up and down like 20 times! It was hilarious and made me laugh!"

- After students return to the classroom, they can share the different things they found and talk about how they feel after sharing. Students will feel uplifted, and you can make the point that there are things that bring us joy around us all the time. We simply have to make a point to notice them!

Around the Room Variation

- For this variation, have students stay in their seats and look around the classroom for things that make them smile.

- Emphasize that these things do not have to be the usual things they might think of that bring joy. They can be very small things, such as the color of a book, a funny inscription on a pen, or a cloud outside the classroom window.

- Give students a time limit to do this. Two minutes generally works well.

- Once they complete this exercise, they can share the different things they found and talk about how they feel after sharing. Students may be surprised to realize that there are so many things around and available to them that can bring them a "moment of joy."

Inquiry

- What stood out to you the most about doing this?

- What was it like for you to experience the outdoors (or the hallway, classroom, etc.) in this way?

- How is this different from the way you usually experience the outdoors (or the hallway, classroom, etc.)?

- How do you feel now after doing this activity?

Agency and Purpose Practices

The following lessons are aimed at strengthening students' agency and clarifying their purpose. You can introduce these practices after helping students clarify their core values—what is truly important to them—in session 11. These practices take the idea of core values one step further by asking students to demonstrate agency—or "take the bull by the horns"—and embrace what they really want to do. This helps them identify a sense of purpose or mission in life.

You can think of agency as a form of "fierce self-compassion" (Neff, 2021). That's because self-compassion is not just about being kind and tender to yourself but also about standing up for what you believe in and engaging in the world. When someone is being threatened, mistreated, or hurt in some way, self-compassion can step in and say, "No! I refuse to be treated this way!" It gives you the courage and agency to stand up for yourself and fight for what you believe in. Our own research shows that teens who are more self-compassionate are able to be more agentic—they are more able to move outside their comfort zone and embrace new experiences (Bluth et al., 2018).

Agency often emerges from a sense of purpose. To find purpose, teens need to know three things—what their values are, what their skills or strengths are, and what the world needs that moves them. That is, once students have brought some clarity to their core values and identified and honored their strengths, they need to turn to the world issues that resonate with them. Is it fighting against school shootings, climate change, lack of adequate health care, or racial injustice? Perhaps an issue in the local community? Knowing their core values—what's fundamentally most important to them—can lead the way. In general, students in middle and high school have some awareness of issues that they feel strongly about, whether it's local rules around the school dress code or global issues like persecution in a fascist government on the other side of the world.

Therefore, after helping students uncover their core values in session 11, this next series of lessons will help them identify what their skills are and honor these skills in a way that drives a sense of agency and purpose.

Discovering My Skills

Intention

- Have students recognize their natural talents

- Allow students to appreciate and focus on the skills that come naturally to them

Instructions

- For this writing exercise, ask students to take out a pen and paper (or journal). Then read the following script to students:

In this exercise, we are going to discover the various skills and talents that we have that come naturally to us. We all have these skills, but the activities we're involved in don't always highlight them, so we may not be aware of them. For example, some people are really good at figuring out how things work mechanically, but since school doesn't focus on this skill, they may not be so aware of it. Others are naturally good at music or speaking in public. It's important to know our natural abilities so that we can build on them if we so choose.

To help you uncover your natural talents, use a pen and paper to respond to the following four questions:

- *What do my friends and the adults around me tell me I'm good at? What do they compliment me for?*

- *What do I do well at in school?*

- *What's pretty easy for me to learn to do?*

- *What kind of activities do I get completely immersed in and forget about everything else around me?*

Discussion

- What was it like to identify your strengths? How did it make you feel?

- Were you surprised at anything you discovered when answering these questions?

- Can you think of any ways to make this skill be a bigger part of your life?

Honoring My Strengths

Intention

- Allow students to savor and appreciate their skills

- Help students appreciate others who have been a part of their journey in developing these skills

Instructions

- This practice is a good follow-up to the *Discovering My Skills* exercise, as it encourages students to take a moment to appreciate their own skills.

- To begin, read the following script to students:

Please close your eyes if that feels right to you, and take a few deep breaths, allowing yourself to settle into the chair you're sitting in. Check to make sure your shoulders are relaxed, the muscles of your face are relaxed, and your belly is relaxed.

Now, take a moment to think about a strength or skill that you have. Something you know that you're good at and that, really deep down, you like about yourself. You won't have to share this with anyone, so please be honest. [Long pause]

Sometimes it's easier to recognize your strengths when you remember that these strengths stem, in large part, from the positive contributions of others in your life.

Are there any people who helped you develop your strengths, maybe friends, parents, teachers, or even authors of books who had a positive impact on you? Maybe characters in a movie or TV series?

As you think of each person, please send them some gratitude and appreciation.

When you honor yourself, you honor those who have helped support you.

Remember, you don't have to be the best in order to appreciate something about yourself. You just need to know in your heart that this is something you're good at and that you like about yourself.

Let yourself savor, just for this moment, this good feeling about yourself. Let it soak in.

When you're ready, you can gently open your eyes if they've been closed.

Inquiry

- How did you feel when doing this practice?

- Was it strange or odd to be honoring your strengths in this way?

- Did any obstacles arise? In other words, did you notice yourself having a hard time doing this practice? Maybe feeling odd or guilty because you were taking time to honor your strengths? [*Remind students that it takes some time for these practices to feel comfortable. They aren't in the habit of treating themselves with kindness and respect. Just like anything that is new—whether it's playing a musical instrument or a sport, for example—it feels weird the first few times until you get used to it.*]

Identifying a Purpose

Intention

- Help students begin to explore local and global issues that are meaningful to them

Instructions

- Ask students to identify the top three issues on the list below that inspire them. (Feel free to add other issues to this list.) Students may want to keep in mind the core values they identified in the *My House/My Self* exercise from session 11:

  - LGBTQIA+ rights

  - Immigration

  - Climate change

  - Cleaning up local parks and other green spaces

  - Quality health care (either local or global)

  - Quality education (either local or global)

  - Animal rights

  - Racial and ethnic equality

  - Arts curriculum in public schools

  - Dress code in public schools

  - Gun control

  - Voting rights

  - Homelessness

  - Supporting veterans

  - Supporting those currently in the military

  - Advancing technology in schools

  - Hunger (either local or global)

  - Rights of the disabled

- Children with special needs

- Children with a chronic illness

- Children with cancer

- Then ask students to respond to the following questions. This can be done in small groups of students who feel similarly about issues or individually.

    - What is it about this issue that grabs your attention?

    - Why is it important to you?

    - What might happen if people like you don't help out?

    - What might happen if people like you do help out?

    - What is the best-case scenario for the outcome of this issue?

    - What is the worst-case scenario for the outcome of this issue?

Discussion

- What have you learned about various issues that might be important to you?

EXERCISE

Planning a Purpose

Intention

- Help students make a plan to engage in local or global issues that are meaningful to them

- Explore how much time and focus students may want to devote to their cause

Instructions

- To help students investigate specific ways they can work toward a cause that supports their values, encourage them to conduct an internet search to find local or global organizations where they can volunteer to support the issue. A good place to start is www.dosomething.org, an organization described as "a youth activism hub fueling young people to change the world."

- Make sure to explore what experience or skills they need to begin their volunteer efforts, if any.

- Have students consider the amount of time per week or per month they want to devote to this issue.

- Finally, encourage them to create a plan for how they will launch their effort to work on this cause.

Discussion

- How would working toward this cause support your core values?

- Notice how you feel when you are thinking about working at this cause. What emotions come up for you? For example, do you feel excited, anxious, overwhelmed, or inspired?

- How might self-compassion help you as you consider working on this issue?

CHAPTER 6

A Final Word to Teachers

> 66 Integrity requires that I discern what is integral to my selfhood,
> what fits and what does not—and that I choose life-giving ways
> of relating to the forces that converge within me: Do I welcome
> them or fear them, embrace them or reject them, move with them
> or against them? By choosing integrity, I become more whole, but
> wholeness does not mean perfection. It means becoming more real
> by acknowledging the whole of who I am.
>
> **—Parker J. Palmer**

You now have everything it takes to teach students how to be kinder to themselves. You have your own self-compassion practice, you have guides for teaching the curriculum, and you have the curriculum itself. And most of all, you have your huge heart that cares about your students and is committed to helping them navigate middle and high school. So have faith that all will unfold as it is supposed to.

That doesn't mean your presentation of the curriculum will be perfect. It won't. You're human, and like all of us, you'll stumble at times and say things that you wish you hadn't. But have no fear—this is an opportunity for you to strengthen your own self-compassion practice! Many times, I've made mistakes and regretted certain things that happened when teaching this curriculum, even after teaching it dozens of times. And you know what? I've turned these mistakes into learning opportunities for the students, and you can too.

Here is one of *many* examples. One time, my phone rang in the middle of class. Instead of berating myself and rushing over to turn it off, I brought the students into my thinking process in real time. I said, "So my phone just rang, right? I have a choice. I can criticize myself and say something like 'What kind of teacher are you?! You should know better than that! Why didn't you turn your phone off before class? How could you forget such an important thing?' Or I can say something like 'That's a perfectly normal human mistake. It happens. You have a lot going on. Maybe next time, leave yourself a reminder somewhere obvious so that you'll remember to turn off your phone.'"

This approach revealed several important lessons to students. First, it was a demonstration of my common humanity—that we all make mistakes, even teachers. Second, it showcased my thinking process and revealed the important fact that anytime we make a mistake, we have a choice—we can either be hard on ourselves, or we can be understanding of ourselves. Notice that in both cases, we aren't letting ourselves off the hook. We are still responsible for making sure our phone is turned off next time before class.

Since we all make mistakes, you don't have to run around trying to cover up your errors and pretend like you're a teacher who has it all together. (I'm not saying that you do that, of course, but I certainly did when I was a classroom teacher!) Instead, use mistakes as an opportunity to demonstrate to your students how you are actively choosing not to be self-critical. Use it as an opportunity to show them that it's possible to take responsibility for mistakes while being encouraging and supportive to yourself. They will internalize this process, and it will help them in their own process of learning to be more self-compassionate.

Questions Others May Have about Self-Compassion

Since our culture does not teach us how to be kind to ourselves, self-compassion is a pretty radical idea that others may understandably have doubts about. These doubts are really misconceptions about what self-compassion is and how it serves us—all of us. So, when you approach your administration or school board about bringing self-compassion into your school, do your homework and be prepared to respond to their questions. Here are some talking points that can quell some of their doubts.

The biggest doubt that people have about self-compassion is that it will destroy motivation and make people lazy. Truth be told, the data show the opposite—people who are more self-compassionate are *more* motivated to try hard and embrace new experiences, even in the face of failure. They're also more likely to take responsibility and apologize when they've done something that they felt was wrong (Breines & Chen, 2012).

Why might this be so? Self-compassionate people aren't as fearful of failure as others. When self-compassionate people fail or make a mistake, they know this doesn't mean they're a hopelessly inadequate, miserable person. They know that imperfection and even failure are parts of being human, so they don't condemn themselves to a lifetime of tragedy. They recognize where they messed up, promise to themselves that they'll proceed differently next time, and move on.

Another misconception that people have about self-compassion is that it's selfish or self-serving. Yet again, research has shown us that the opposite is true. People who are more self-compassionate have more to give because their *own* emotional needs are being met. In fact, one study found that self-compassionate people are more caring, accepting, and supporting toward their partners, whereas those who are more self-critical come across as detached, aggressive, and controlling toward their partners (Neff & Beretvas, 2013). I don't have to tell you which relationships were stronger overall! These findings make sense, because when attending to your own needs with kindness and care, you feel more supported and grounded to care for others in turn.

Finally, some people are afraid that self-compassion will result in self-pity. They fear that if we teach students to be kinder to themselves, they'll withdraw into their bedrooms amid a torrent of tears, weeping about "poor me." Yet self-compassion includes the critical component of common humanity, which recognizes that whatever painful emotions befall us, we are not alone. Emotional pain—whether it's anger, loneliness, hurt, depression, anxiety, or sadness—is part of being human. These are emotional experiences we all share, and self-compassion allows us to see this thread of common humanity instead of feeling sorry for ourselves. This is often particularly eye-opening for teens, who often see themselves as the only ones experiencing emotional pain. They are often surprised when they realize that others also are experiencing these difficult emotions.

Building a Self-Compassionate School Community

Once you're off and running with your program, you may find that others start noticing slight changes in your students and start asking about what's going on in your classroom. The first step to respond to their queries is to explain what self-compassion is all about. This can happen at parent-teacher conferences, PTA meetings, schoolwide in-service workshops, and other similar venues. Once the school community has an understanding of self-compassion, and any doubts about it have been addressed, the next step is to encourage others to cultivate compassion in themselves by taking self-compassion courses. Thousands of self-compassion instructors have been trained worldwide, and courses are available online and in person. Appendix 1 includes a list of these resources.

Parents who take self-compassion courses will be able to better support their children as they learn self-compassion in the classroom and will be in a more grounded place to handle the often rocky path of parenting teenagers. School staff who take these courses will also be in a better place to support students and have the steadiness to deal with the day-to-day challenges of working in a school setting.

We all struggle with the challenges of living in a divisive, often anger-fueled 21st-century society, where we are expected to juggle multiple competing responsibilities. In this contentious climate, your ability to share self-compassion with everyone in your school community—whether it's administrators, maintenance workers, parents, bus drivers, or cafeteria workers—will strengthen the foundation of your school community.

This book will start you on this journey. Keep it with you, begin with your own self-compassion practice, and then take it one small step at a time. You have everything you need to venture on this path. Trust yourself, be authentic, include yourself in your circle of compassion, and delight in the fruits that follow.

PART 3

Appendices

APPENDIX 1

Supplementary Resources

Self-Compassion Books for Teens

- *The Self-Compassion Workbook for Teens: Mindfulness and Compassion Skills to Overcome Self-Criticism and Embrace Who You Are* by Karen Bluth

- *The Self-Compassionate Teen: Mindfulness and Compassion Skills to Conquer Your Critical Inner Voice* by Karen Bluth

- *Mindfulness and Self-Compassion for Teen ADHD: Build Executive Functioning Skills, Increase Motivation, and Improve Self-Confidence* by Mark Bertin and Karen Bluth

- *The Mindful Teen: Powerful Skills to Help You Handle Stress One Moment at a Time* by Dzung X. Vo

Self-Compassion Books for Educators

- *Self-Compassion for Educators: Mindful Practices to Awaken Your Well-Being and Grow Resilience* by Lisa Baylis

- *Self-Compassion for Girls: A Guide for Parents, Teachers, and Coaches* by Karen Bluth (an Audible Original)

- *The Mindful Self-Compassion Workbook: A Proven Way to Accept Yourself, Build Inner Strength, and Thrive* by Kristin Neff and Christopher Germer

- *Self-Compassion: The Proven Power of Being Kind to Yourself* by Kristin Neff

- *The Mindful Path to Self-Compassion: Freeing Yourself from Destructive Thoughts and Emotions* by Christopher Germer

- *Fierce Self-Compassion: How Women Can Harness Kindness to Speak Up, Claim Their Power, and Thrive* by Kristin Neff
- *Self-Compassion for Dummies* by Steven Hickman

Mindfulness Books

- *Trauma-Sensitive Mindfulness: Practices for Safe and Transformative Healing* by David A. Treleaven
- *10% Happier: How I Tamed the Voice in My Head, Reduced Stress Without Losing My Edge, and Found Self-Help That Actually Works—A True Story* by Dan Harris
- *Meditation for Fidgety Skeptics: A 10% Happier How-To Book* by Dan Harris
- *Wherever You Go, There You Are: Mindfulness Meditation in Everyday Life* by Jon Kabat-Zinn
- *Brainstorm: The Power and Purpose of the Teenage Brain* by Daniel J. Siegel

Websites

- www.lisabaylis.com: Lisa is the author of the book *Self-Compassion for Educators*, and her website includes information for several retreats and courses that educators can take on the topic of self-compassion.
- www.karenbluth.com: My website includes information about my research and publications, as well as a bit about my own mindfulness and self-compassion journey.
- www.centerformsc.org: The Center for Mindful Self-Compassion, founded by Kristin Neff and Christopher Germer, manages the international Mindful Self-Compassion program. The website includes information about self-compassion courses held internationally, as well as teacher trainings for both the adult and teen mindful self-compassion courses.
- www.self-compassion.org: Kristin Neff has many resources on her website, including a compilation of research studies, YouTube talks, audio and video recordings of guided practices, and self-compassion scales.
- www.chrisgermer.com: Christopher Germer includes several resources on his website, including workshops, online programs, and audio recordings of guided practices.

Worksheets to Accompany the Curriculum

Session 1: Discovering Mindful Self-Compassion

After completing the *Sunbathing* practice, answer one or more of the questions below. You can use the emotion wheel to help you figure out what you are feeling. There is no right or wrong way to feel—all answers are welcome!

- What did it feel like to imagine having the sun on your face?

- What was it like when I said, "Everything is going to be okay"?

- Did you notice anything else?

_____

_____

_____

_____

_____

_____

_____

After completing the *Compassionate Friend* practice, answer one or more of the questions below. You can write or draw your response.

- Were you able to find a place that felt safe and comfortable?

- Were you able to identify a compassionate friend?

- What is it like to know that you have this compassionate friend inside you at all times?

Reflection

Draw or write your response to these questions:

- What stands out to you about this first class?

- What do you think this program is going to be like?

<u>WORKSHEET</u>

Session 2: Being Kind to Myself

After completing the *How Would I Treat a Friend* exercise, answer one or more of the questions below. You can write or draw your response.

- What did you learn about yourself in this exercise?

- What were the differences in how you treated a friend versus how you treated yourself?

- What was it like to realize that?

Reflection

Draw or write your response to this question:

- What is one way you can integrate what you learned in class into your daily life?

Session 3: Paying Attention on Purpose

After finishing *Drawing My Safe Place*, how do you feel? Use the emotion wheel to help you identify what you're feeling.

_____

_____

_____

_____

_____

_____

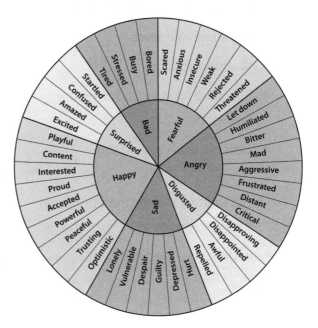

Reflection

Draw or write your response to these questions:

- What is mindfulness as you understand it?

- How might practicing mindfulness help you in your life?

Session 4: Mindfulness

Choose an activity to do mindfully every day for the next week:

- Brushing your teeth
- Washing your face
- Reaching for your phone before answering a text
- Eating a few bites of food
- Listening fully to a friend, teacher, classmate, or family member when they are speaking
- Petting your cat or dog

- Kicking a soccer ball around
- Taking a shower
- Listening to a piece of music
- Drawing
- Playing a musical instrument
- Shooting baskets
- Brushing your hair
- _____

Reflection

Many teens have expressed the different ways that their here-and-now stone has helped reduce anxiety and stress. Draw or write your response to these questions:

- When do you think you will use your here-and-now stone?
- How do you think it will help you?
- If you don't have a here-and-now stone, what object could you use instead?

Session 5: The Adolescent Brain

After completing the *Affectionate Breathing* or *Three Soothing Breaths* practices, answer one or more of the questions below. You can write or draw your response.

- Were you able to feel your breath, even for a second?

- What was that like? Did you discover anything new about your breath (e.g., that it's smooth, bumpy, warm, or cold)?

- Did your mind wander? What did you do when you noticed it had wandered?

Reflection

In this session, you learned that the brain is changing more during the teen years than at any other time except for infancy, and that these changes often affect your behavior.

Draw or write your response to this question:

- How can this knowledge help you be kinder to yourself?

Session 6: Kindness

After completing the *Kindness for Someone You Care About* practice, answer one or more of the questions below. You can use the emotion wheel to help you figure out what you are feeling.

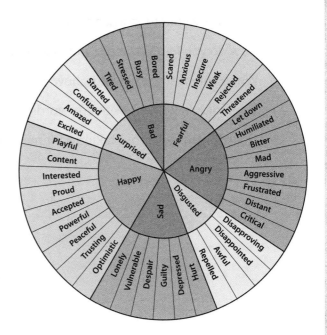

- What was it like to wish good things for someone else?

- What was it like to wish good things for both someone else and yourself?

- How about when you were just wishing good things for yourself? What was that like?

- Did you have difficulty feeling kindness with this practice, either to yourself or the other being? If you had difficulty being kind to yourself, no worries! You're not yet in the habit, and it takes time to develop a new habit.

_____

_____

_____

_____

_____

_____

_____

_____

_____

_____

Reflection

Often, it takes some time to find kind words or phrases that work for us, as these words can be very personal and reflect a need that may not be so obvious to us at first.

Draw or write your response to these questions:

- How do you feel about the words you came up with? Did they feel true to you?

- When you hear those words, how do you feel?

- If you didn't come up with any words, how did that feel?

- How do you feel about taking a bit more time to come up with the right words?

Session 7: Laying the Foundation for Self-Compassion

After completing the *Calming Music* practice, answer one or more of the questions below. You can use the emotion wheel to help you figure out what you are feeling.

- What was this practice like for you?

- How did your body feel after the practice?

- Did you notice your mind wandering? Were you able to bring it back?

- Did you observe any self-judgment when you noticed your mind was wandering?

- Did you notice any reactions to the music, either pleasant or unpleasant? How did you know?

- How do you think you can incorporate this music practice into your life?

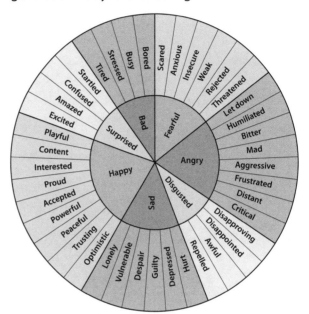

_____

_____

_____

_____

_____

_____

_____

_____

_____

Reflection

Draw or write your response to this question:

- What do you think your school would be like if everyone, including teachers, school staff, and school administration, did the *A Person Just Like Me* practice for a different person each day?

Session 8: Self-Compassion

After completing the *Motivating Ourselves with Compassion* exercise, answer one or more of the questions below:

- How well were you able to hear your inner critic? Circle one. Then write or draw more about this experience.

- How well were you able to hear your compassionate voice? Circle one. Then write or draw more about this experience.

- If you heard it, how helpful was it to hear your compassionate voice (where 0 is "not helpful at all" and 10 is "extremely helpful")?

 ——————————————————————————
　　　　1　　2　　3　　4　　5　　6　　7　　8　　9　　10

Reflection

In this session, we learned that our inner critic often starts out with a positive intention. Maybe it is trying to keep us safe, motivate us, or help us avoid things that might hurt us.

Draw or write your response to these questions:

- How might this knowledge help you in the future?

- How would it be to allow your inner critic's voice to still be around without necessarily listening to it?

Session 9: Self-Compassion vs. Self-Esteem

Before beginning the *Social Media Exploration* exercise, respond to the question below:

- How do you feel? Use the emotion wheel to identify what you are feeling. Then use the scale below to indicate how strongly you feel this emotion (where 0 is "very little" and 10 is "the most you can feel that emotion").

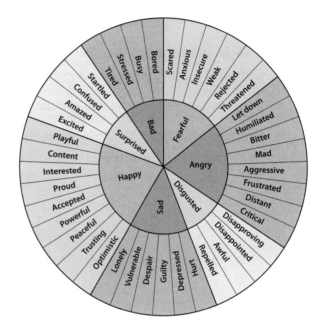

_____

_____

_____

_____

_____

    1   2   3   4   5   6   7   8   9   10

After completing the *Social Media Exploration* exercise, respond to the questions below:

- How do you feel? Use the emotion wheel to identify what you are feeling. Then use the scale below to indicate how strongly you feel this emotion (where 0 is "very little" and 10 is "the most you can feel that emotion").

_____

_____

    1   2   3   4   5   6   7   8   9   10

- Were you able to offer yourself compassion, even a little, for any self-criticism that arose during the exercise?

_____

_____

Reflection

Draw or write your response to these questions:

- If social media made you feel worse, do you think you can still use social media without it hurting you or making you feel badly?

- If so, what are some ways you can make this happen?

- If you felt the same or better after the exercise, how can you support yourself if there's a time in the future when you feel worse after using social media?

Session 10: Common Humanity

After completing the *Crossing the Line* exercise, answer one or more of the questions below:

- How surprising was it that so many others "crossed the line" with you (where 0 is "not surprising at all" and 10 is "extremely surprising")?

1   2   3   4   5   6   7   8   9   10

- How might you feel learning that others experienced similar things to you? You can use the emotion wheel to help you figure out what you are feeling.

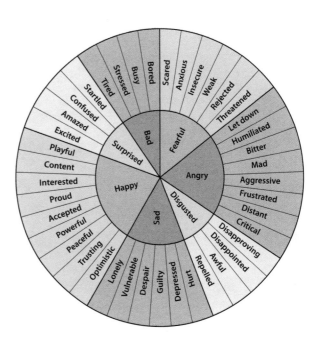

_____

_____

_____

_____

_____

Reflection

In the *Japanese Bowls* exercise, we learned that (1) going through difficult experiences often makes us stronger, and (2) what we see as our "flaws" or "imperfections" are really what make us interesting and unique. Think about how one (or both) of these two things can be true in your own life and write or draw about it here.

Session 11: Core Values

After completing the *My House/My Self* exercise, what obstacles did you find that stand in the way of living by your core values?

- Peer pressure
- Fear of failure
- Insecurity
- Lack of money
- Not having a car
- Your parents/caregivers

- Being shy
- Being a teenager and not being able to do what you want
- _____
- _____
- _____

Reflection

Like all human beings, we will stray from our core values from time to time. When this happens, we may find ourselves feeling inauthentic, as if we are living by somebody else's needs or desires. Draw or write your response to this question:

- How can being self-compassionate help when this happens?

Session 12: Silver Linings

After completing the *Giving and Receiving Compassion* practice, respond to one or more of the questions below:

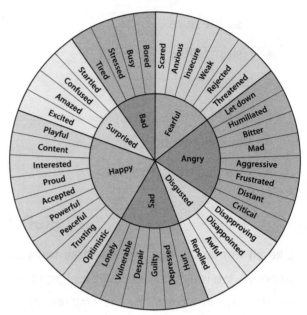

- How did you feel when you gave compassion to yourself? Use the emotion wheel to identify what you are feeling. Then use the scale below to indicate how strongly you feel this emotion (where 0 is "very little" and 10 is "the most you can feel that emotion").

_____

_____

_____

_____

 _____ 1   2   3   4   5   6   7   8   9   10

- How did you feel when you gave compassion to others? Again, use the emotion wheel to identify what you are feeling. Then use the scale below to indicate how strongly you feel this emotion (where 0 is "very little" and 10 is "the most you can feel that emotion").

_____

_____

 _____ 1   2   3   4   5   6   7   8   9   10

- Was it easier to give compassion to yourself or another? (Remember, if it was easier giving to others, it's because you've been doing that your whole life! Giving yourself compassion is something new and takes some time to get used to.)

_____

_____

After the *Silver Linings* exercise, respond to one or more of the questions below:

- What did you learn from this exercise?
- How do you feel after completing this exercise?

_____

_____

_____

Reflection

In this session, we discovered that we often learn important lessons when we go through difficult times in our lives. Draw or write your response to this question:

- Can you think of any struggles you are going through right now that perhaps, in the future, you'll look back on and realize that you learned something important from?

Session 13: Getting to Know Difficult Emotions

After completing the *Soften, Support, Open* practice, answer one or more of the questions below:

- Did you notice a change or shift when you *labeled* the emotion associated with situation?

_____

_____

_____

- If you were able to find where the emotion "lives" in your body, where was it? (Circle the location.)

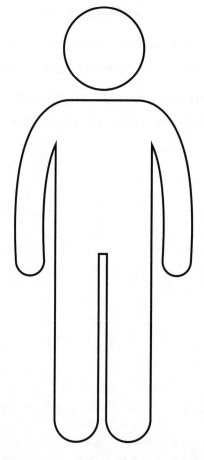

- Did the emotion change when you *softened* that part of the body, *supported* yourself, and *opened* to it being there?

_____

_____

_____

Reflection

When we experience difficult emotions such as anger, sadness, loneliness, grief, disappointment, and hurt, we often feel tight and constricted. Draw or write your response to this question:

- What did playing with oobleck show you about how to work with difficult emotions?

Session 14: Anger and the Adolescent Brain

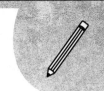

After completing the *Exploring Unmet Needs* practice, answer one or more of the questions below:

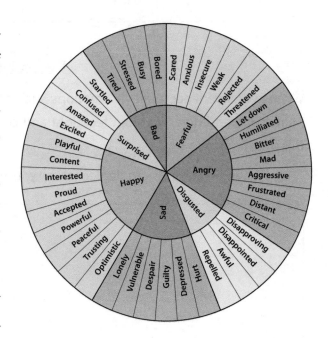

- How did it feel to validate your anger? Use the emotion wheel to identify what you are feeling. Then use the scale below to indicate how strongly you feel this emotion (where 0 is "very little" and 10 is "the most you can feel that emotion").

_____

_____

 1   2   3   4   5   6   7   8   9   10

- Could you find the softer, more vulnerable feelings underneath the anger, such as fear, sadness, or hurt?

_____

_____

- Were you able to identify an unmet need underneath the softer, more vulnerable feelings? This might include the need to belong, the need to be heard, or the need to be loved.

_____

_____

- Were you able to say some kind words to yourself to meet that need, even just a little? Remember, don't worry if you weren't able to this time. Sometimes these practices take time!

- How do you feel now? Use the emotion wheel to identify what you are feeling. Then use the scale below to indicate how strongly you feel this emotion (where 0 is "very little" and 10 is "the most you can feel that emotion").

---

    1   2   3   4   5   6   7   8   9   10

Reflection

In this session, we learned that there are two systems in the brain that are undergoing development during the teen years—the prefrontal cortex (which is responsible for logical thinking and decision-making) and the limbic system (which is responsible for our emotions). Draw or write your response to this question:

- Knowing that the emotional part of your brain finishes developing way before the logical thinking part of your brain, how can this information help you understand yourself better and be more self-compassionate?

Session 15: Embracing Your Life with Gratitude

After listening mindfully to soothing music in the *Calming Music* practice, respond to one or more of the questions below:

- How do you feel now? Use the emotion wheel to identify what you are feeling. Then use the scale below to indicate how strongly you feel this emotion (where 0 is "very little" and 10 is "the most you can feel that emotion").

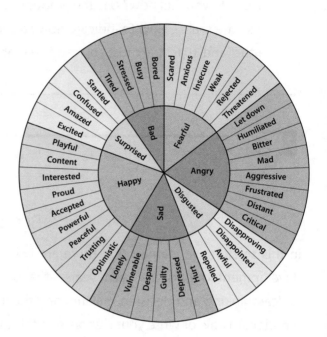

_____

_____

 1   2   3   4   5   6   7   8   9   10

- What did you do when you noticed your mind wandering?

_____

_____

- Did you observe any self-judgment when you noticed your mind was wandering? What did you do?

_____

_____

Reflection

Gratitude has been tied to both physical and mental health in many research studies. Draw or write your response to this question:

- Why do you think the practice of noticing the good things in life leads to better overall well-being?

Session 16: Maintaining the Practice

After completing the *Compassionate Friend* practice in the final session, answer the question below:

- How was the *Compassionate Friend* practice the same or different from when you completed it in the first session?

_____

_____

Reflection

Draw or write your response to this question:

- We so often forget to appreciate the good things about ourselves. Why do you think this is so?

APPENDIX 3

Assessments

The scales included here can be administered before and after the program to determine students' progress. You can use any or all of them, depending on what you are interested in assessing. For example, if you aren't interested in determining whether students are more satisfied with their lives after the program is over, there's no need to include that scale.

Scale 1. Perceived Stress Scale (Cohen et al., 1983): This scale measures how stressed a student perceives themselves to be. To score, add up the total number of points for all 10 items. A higher score indicates higher stress.

Scale 2. Student Life Satisfaction Scale (Huebner, 1991): This scale measures how satisfied a student is with their life. To score, add up the total number of points for all 7 items. A higher score indicates higher life satisfaction.

Scale 3. Youth Self-Compassion Scale (Neff et al., 2021): This scale measures how self-compassionate a student is. To score, add up the total number of points for all 17 items. A higher score indicates higher self-compassion.

Scale 4. Difficulties in Emotion Regulation Scale-16 (Bjureberg et al., 2016): This scale measures the challenges that a student has in regulating their emotions, which is often linked with behavior challenges in the classroom. To score, add up the total number of points for all 16 items. A higher score indicates greater emotion regulation difficulties.

Note that these scales have been slightly modified from the original validated versions so they are easier for teachers to score and therefore shouldn't be used for research purposes. The names of the scales have been intentionally omitted on the pages that follow so they can be copied and distributed to students.

Scale 1

The questions in this scale ask about your feelings and thoughts over the last month. Although some questions seem similar, there are differences between them, so you should treat each one as a separate question. The best approach is to answer fairly quickly. That is, don't try to count up the number of times you felt a particular way—just circle the answer that seems like a reasonable estimate. **Pay careful attention to the answers in each question, as the scale is reversed in some instances (where *never* is rated a 5 and *very often* is a 1).**

In the last month . . .	1	2	3	4	5
How often have you been upset because of something that happened unexpectedly?	Never	Almost never	Sometimes	Fairly often	Very often
How often have you felt that you were unable to control the important things in your life?	Never	Almost never	Sometimes	Fairly often	Very often
How often have you felt nervous and stressed?	Never	Almost never	Sometimes	Fairly often	Very often
How often have you felt confident about your ability to handle your personal problems?	Very often	Fairly often	Sometimes	Almost never	Never
How often have you felt that things were going your way?	Very often	Fairly often	Sometimes	Almost never	Never

In the last month . . .	1	2	3	4	5
How often have you found that you could not cope with all the things that you had to do?	Never	Almost never	Sometimes	Fairly often	Very often
How often have you been able to control irritations in your life?	Very often	Fairly often	Sometimes	Almost never	Never
How often have you felt that you were on top of things?	Very often	Fairly often	Sometimes	Almost never	Never
How often have you been angered because of things that happened that were outside of your control?	Never	Almost never	Sometimes	Fairly often	Very often
How often have you felt difficulties were piling up so high that you could not overcome them?	Never	Almost never	Sometimes	Fairly often	Very often

Scale 2

The questions in this scale ask you to think about your overall satisfaction with life over the past several weeks. Circle the answer that best describes the extent to which you agree or disagree with each statement. **Pay careful attention to the answers in each question, as the scale is reversed in some instances (where *never* is rated a 5 and *almost always* is a 1).**

	1	2	3	4
My life is going well.	Never	Sometimes	Often	Almost always
My life is just right.	Never	Sometimes	Often	Almost always
I would like to change many things in my life.	Almost always	Often	Sometimes	Never
I wish I had a different kind of life.	Almost always	Often	Sometimes	Never
I have a good life.	Never	Sometimes	Often	Almost always
I have what I want in life.	Never	Sometimes	Often	Almost always
My life is better than most kids'.	Never	Sometimes	Often	Almost always

Scale 3

The questions in this scale ask you to think about how you typically act toward yourself in difficult times. **Pay careful attention to the answers in each question, as the scale is reversed in some instances (where *almost never* is rated a 5 and *almost always* is a 1).**

	1	2	3	4	5
I try to be kind and supportive to myself when I'm having a hard time.	Almost never	Not very often	Sometimes	Very often	Almost always
When I feel sad or down, it seems like I'm the only one who feels this way.	Almost always	Very often	Sometimes	Not very often	Almost never
When I notice things about myself that I don't like, I get really frustrated.	Almost always	Very often	Sometimes	Not very often	Almost never
When I feel I'm not "good enough" in some way, I try to remind myself that other people sometimes feel this way too.	Almost never	Not very often	Sometimes	Very often	Almost always
When I feel frustrated or disappointed, I think about it over and over again.	Almost always	Very often	Sometimes	Not very often	Almost never

	1	2	3	4	5
When something upsetting happens, I try to see things as they are without blowing it out of proportion.	Almost never	Not very often	Sometimes	Very often	Almost always
I get mad at myself for not being better at some things.	Almost always	Very often	Sometimes	Not very often	Almost never
When I'm sad or unhappy, I remember that other people also feel this way at times.	Almost never	Not very often	Sometimes	Very often	Almost always
I'm kind to myself when things go wrong and I'm feeling bad.	Almost never	Not very often	Sometimes	Very often	Almost always
When I feel bad or upset, I tend to feel most other people are probably happier than I am.	Almost always	Very often	Sometimes	Not very often	Almost never
When something difficult happens, I try to see things clearly without exaggerations.	Almost never	Not very often	Sometimes	Very often	Almost always

	1	2	3	4	5
I'm really hard on myself when I do something wrong.	Almost always	Very often	Sometimes	Not very often	Almost never
When things aren't going well, I keep in mind that life is sometimes hard for everyone.	Almost never	Not very often	Sometimes	Very often	Almost always
When I'm feeling bad or upset, I can't think of anything else at the time.	Almost always	Very often	Sometimes	Not very often	Almost never
I try to be understanding and patient with myself even when I mess up.	Almost never	Not very often	Sometimes	Very often	Almost always
When I'm really struggling, I tend to feel like other people are probably having an easier time of it.	Almost always	Very often	Sometimes	Not very often	Almost never
When something upsets me, I try to notice my feelings and not get carried away by them.	Almost never	Not very often	Sometime	Very often	Almost always

Scale 4

Please indicate how often the following statements apply to you. Circle the response that is true for you.

	1	2	3	4	5
I have difficulty making sense out of my feelings.	Almost never	Sometimes	About half the time	Most of the time	Almost always
I am confused about how I feel.	Almost never	Sometimes	About half the time	Most of the time	Almost always
When I am upset, I have difficulty getting work done.	Almost never	Sometimes	About half the time	Most of the time	Almost always
When I am upset, I become out of control.	Almost never	Sometimes	About half the time	Most of the time	Almost always
When I am upset, I believe that I will remain that way for a long time.	Almost never	Sometimes	About half the time	Most of the time	Almost always
When I am upset, I believe that I'll end up feeling very depressed.	Almost never	Sometimes	About half the time	Most of the time	Almost always

	1	2	3	4	5
When I am upset, I have difficulty focusing on other things.	Almost never	Sometimes	About half the time	Most of the time	Almost always
When I am upset, I feel out of control.	Almost never	Sometimes	About half the time	Most of the time	Almost always
When I am upset, I feel ashamed with myself for feeling that way.	Almost never	Sometimes	About half the time	Most of the time	Almost always
When I am upset, I feel like I am weak.	Almost never	Sometimes	About half the time	Most of the time	Almost always
When I am upset, I have difficulty controlling my behaviors.	Almost never	Sometimes	About half the time	Most of the time	Almost always
When I am upset, I believe that there is nothing I can do to make myself feel better.	Almost never	Sometimes	About half the time	Most of the time	Almost always

	1	2	3	4	5
When I am upset, I become irritated with myself for feeling that way.	Almost never	Sometimes	About half the time	Most of the time	Almost always
When I am upset, I start to feel very bad about myself.	Almost never	Sometimes	About half the time	Most of the time	Almost always
When I am upset, I have difficulty thinking about anything else.	Almost never	Sometimes	About half the time	Most of the time	Almost always
When I am upset, my emotions feel overwhelming.	Almost never	Sometimes	About half the time	Most of the time	Almost always

References

For your convenience, the exercises in this book are available for download at **www.pesipubs.com/MSCIS.**

You can also find recordings of the formal guided practices at **https://karenbluth.com/msct-in-schools.** Or use the QR code:

Bjureberg, J., Ljótsson, B., Tull, M. T., Hedman, E., Sahlin, H., Lundh, L.-G., Bjärehed, J., DiLillo, D., Messman-Moore, T., Gumpert, C. H., & Gratz, K. L. (2016). Development and validation of a brief version of the difficulties in emotion regulation scale: The DERS-16. *Journal of Psychopathology and Behavioral Assessment, 38,* 284–296. https://doi.org/10.1007/s10862-015-9514-x

Bluth, K., Campo, R. A., Futch, W. S., & Gaylord, S. A. (2017). Age and gender differences in the associations of self-compassion and emotional well-being in a large adolescent sample. *Journal of Youth and Adolescence, 46*(4), 840–853. https://doi.org/10.1007/s10964-016-0567-2

Bluth, K., Campo, R. A., Pruteanu-Malinici, S., Reams, A., Mullarkey, M., & Broderick, P. C. (2016). A school-based mindfulness pilot study for ethnically diverse at-risk adolescents. *Mindfulness, 7,* 90–104. https://doi.org/10.1007/s12671-014-0376-1

Bluth, K., & Eisenlohr-Moul, T. A. (2017). Response to a mindful self-compassion intervention in teens: A within-person association of mindfulness, self-compassion, and emotional well-being outcomes. *Journal of Adolescence, 57,* 108–118. https://doi.org/10.1016/j.adolescence.2017.04.001

Bluth, K., Gaylord, S. A., Campo, R. A., Mullarkey, M. C., & Hobbs, L. (2016). Making friends with yourself: A mixed methods pilot study of a mindful self-compassion program for adolescents. *Mindfulness, 7*(2), 479–492. https://doi.org/10.1007/s12671-015-0476-6

Bluth, K., Lathren, C., Clepper-Faith, M., Larson, L. M., Ogunbamowo, D. O., & Pflum, S. (2023). Improving mental health among transgender adolescents: Implementing mindful self-compassion for teens. *Journal of Adolescent Research, 38*(2), 271–302. https://doi.org/10.1177/07435584211062126

Bluth, K., Mullarkey, M., & Lathren, C. (2018). Self-compassion: A potential path to adolescent resilience and positive exploration. *Journal of Child and Family Studies, 27,* 3037–3047. https://doi.org/10.1007/s10826-018-1125-1

Breines, J. G., & Chen, S. (2012). Self-compassion increases self-improvement motivation. *Personality and Social Psychology Bulletin, 38*(9), 1133–1143. https://doi.org/10.1177/0146167212445599

Cohen, S., Kamarck, T., & Mermelstein, R. (1983). A global measure of perceived stress. *Journal of Health and Social Behavior, 24*(4), 385–396. https://doi.org/10.2307/2136404

Devaney, E., O'Brien, M. U., Resnik, H., Keister, S., & Weissberg, R. P. (2006). *Sustainable schoolwide social and emotional learning (SEL): Implementation guide and toolkit.* Collaborative for Academic, Social, and Emotional Learning (NJ3).

Elkind, D. (1967). Egocentrism in adolescence. *Child Development, 38*(4), 1025–1034. https://doi.org/10.2307/1127100

Felver, J. C., & Singh, N. N. (2020). *Mindfulness in the classroom: An evidence-based program to reduce disruptive behavior and increase academic engagement.* New Harbinger Publications.

Fredrickson, B. L., Arizmendi, C., Van Cappellen, P., Firestine, A. M., Brantley, M. M., Kim, S. L., Brantley, J., & Salzberg, S. (2019). Do contemplative moments matter? Effects of informal meditation on emotions and perceived social integration. *Mindfulness, 10*(9), 1915–1925. https://doi.org/10.1007/s12671-019-01154-2

Fritz, M. M., Armenta, C. N., Walsh, L. C., & Lyubomirsky, S. (2019). Gratitude facilitates healthy eating behavior in adolescents and young adults. *Journal of Experimental Social Psychology, 81*, 4–14. https://doi.org/10.1016/j.jesp.2018.08.011

Froh, J. J., Kashdan, T. B., Ozimkowski, K. M., & Miller, N. (2009). Who benefits the most from a gratitude intervention in children and adolescents? Examining positive affect as a moderator. *The Journal of Positive Psychology, 4*(5), 408–422. https://doi.org/10.1080/17439760902992464

Germer, C., & Neff, K. (2019). *Teaching the mindful self-compassion program: A guide for professionals.* Guilford Press.

Huebner, E. S. (1991). Initial development of the student's life satisfaction scale. *School Psychology International, 12*(3), 231–240. https://doi.org/10.1177/0143034391123010

Kabat-Zinn, J. (1994). *Wherever you go, there you are: Mindfulness meditation in everyday life.* Hyperion.

Kakoschke, N., Hassed, C., Chambers, R., & Lee, K. (2021). The importance of formal versus informal mindfulness practice for enhancing psychological wellbeing and study engagement in a medical student cohort with a 5-week mindfulness-based lifestyle program. *PLoS One, 16*(10), Article e0258999. https://doi.org/10.1371/journal.pone.0258999

Keutler, M., & McHugh, L. (2022). Self-compassion buffers the effects of perfectionistic self-presentation on social media on wellbeing. *Journal of Contextual Behavioral Science, 23*, 53–58. https://doi.org/10.1016/j.jcbs.2021.11.006

Killingsworth, M. A., & Gilbert, D. T. (2010). A wandering mind is an unhappy mind. *Science, 330*(6006), 932. https://doi.org/10.1126/science.1192439

Knox, M., & Neff, K. (2016, June 16–19). *Comparing compassion for self and others: Impacts on personal and interpersonal well-being* [Paper presentation]. Association for Contextual Behavioral Science 14th Annual World Conference, Seattle, WA, United States.

Lathren, C., Bluth, K., & Park, J. (2019). Adolescent self-compassion moderates the relationship between perceived stress and internalizing symptoms. *Personality and Individual Differences, 143*, 36–41. https://doi.org/10.1016/j.paid.2019.02.008

Manigault, A. W., Slutsky, J., Raye, J., & Creswell, J. D. (2021). Examining practice effects in a randomized controlled trial: Daily life mindfulness practice predicts stress buffering effects of mindfulness meditation training. *Mindfulness, 12*(10), 2487–2497. https://doi.org/10.1007/s12671-021-01718-1

Marsh, I. C., Chan, S. W. Y., & MacBeth, A. (2018). Self-compassion and psychological distress in adolescents—a meta-analysis. *Mindfulness, 9*(4), 1011–1027. https://doi.org/10.1007/s12671-017-0850-7

Marshall, S. L., Parker, P. D., Ciarrochi, J., Sahdra, B., Jackson, C. J., & Heaven, P. C. L. (2015). Self-compassion protects against the negative effects of low self-esteem: A longitudinal study in a large adolescent sample. *Personality and Individual Differences, 74*, 116–121. https://doi.org/10.1016/j.paid.2014.09.013

Neff, K. D. (2003). Self-compassion: An alternative conceptualization of a healthy attitude toward oneself. *Self and Identity, 2*, 85–102. https://doi.org/10.1080/15298860309032

Neff, K. D. (2021). *Fierce self-compassion: How women can harness kindness to speak up, claim their power, and thrive*. Penguin.

Neff, K. D., & Beretvas, S. N. (2013). The role of self-compassion in romantic relationships. *Self and Identity, 12*(1), 78–98. https://doi.org/10.1080/15298868.2011.639548

Neff, K. D., Bluth, K., Tóth-Király, I., Davidson, O., Knox, M. C., Williamson, Z., & Costigan, A. (2021). Development and validation of the Self-Compassion Scale for Youth. *Journal of Personality Assessment, 103*(1), 92–105. https://doi.org/10.1080/00223891.2020.1729774

Phillips, W. J., & Wisniewski, A. T. (2021). Self-compassion moderates the predictive effects of social media use profiles on depression and anxiety. *Computers in Human Behavior Reports, 4*, Article 100128. https://doi.org/10.1016/j.chbr.2021.100128

Pullmer, R., Chung, J., Samson, L., Balanji, S., & Zaitsoff, S. (2019). A systematic review of the relation between self-compassion and depressive symptoms in adolescents. *Journal of Adolescence, 74*, 210–220. https://doi.org/10.1016/j.adolescence.2019.06.006

Sexton, J. B., & Adair, K. C. (2019). Forty-five good things: A prospective pilot study of the three good things well-being intervention in the USA for healthcare worker emotional exhaustion, depression, work–life balance and happiness. *BMJ Open, 9*(3), Article e022695. http://dx.doi.org/10.1136/bmjopen-2018-022695

Shankland, R., Tessier, D., Strub, L., Gauchet, A., & Baeyens, C. (2021). Improving mental health and well-being through informal mindfulness practices: An intervention study. *Applied Psychology: Health and Well-Being, 13*(1), 63–83. https://doi.org/10.1111/aphw.12216

Siegel, D. J. (2010). *The mindful therapist: A clinician's guide to mindsight and neural integration.* W. W. Norton.

Tan, C.-M. (2014). *Search inside yourself: The unexpected path to achieving success, happiness (and world peace).* HarperCollins.

Wong, Y. J., Owen, J., Gabana, N. T., Brown, J. W., McInnis, S., Toth, P., & Gilman, L. (2018). Does gratitude writing improve the mental health of psychotherapy clients? Evidence from a randomized controlled trial. *Psychotherapy Research, 28*(2), 192–202. https://doi.org/10.1080/10503307.2016 .1169332

Xavier, A., Pinto-Gouveia, J., & Cunha, M. (2016). The protective role of self-compassion on risk factors for non-suicidal self-injury in adolescence. *School Mental Health, 8*(4), 476–485. https://doi.org/10.1007 /s12310-016-9197-9

Zhang, H., Chi, P., Long, H., & Ren, X. (2019). Bullying victimization and depression among left-behind children in rural China: Roles of self-compassion and hope. *Child Abuse & Neglect, 96*, Article 104072. https://doi.org/10.1016/j.chiabu.2019.104072

Zhang, Y., Luo, X., Che, X., & Duan, W. (2016). Protective effect of self-compassion to emotional response among students with chronic academic stress. *Frontiers in Psychology, 7*, Article 1802. https://doi.org/10 .3389/fpsyg.2016.01802

Acknowledgments

This book would not be possible without the support and wisdom of so many people. First, my work is built on the ingenuity, determination, and huge hearts of Chris Germer and Kristin Neff, who created the Mindful Self-Compassion program for adults. The curriculum in this book has been adapted from that brilliant and creative work, which has improved the lives of so many people around the world. This curriculum would not exist without their momentous work.

Second, many trained teachers of Mindful Self-Compassion for Teens have contributed to modifications made from the previous version of this program called Making Friends with Yourself, which was co-created by Lorraine Hobbs and myself. Huge thanks to Marina Barnes, Dom Sullivan, Lea Christo, Laura Prochnow Phillips, Kristie Engel, Heather Montague, Skip Hudson, Deidre Hughes, and Jamie Lynn Tatera for the invaluable wisdom, effort, and creativity they put forth toward the teen self-compassion program on which this school curriculum is based. I so appreciate and value each one of you, and am continually moved by your commitment to bringing self-compassion to teens. And huge thanks especially to Lea Christo and Mary Anne Mariani for encouraging me to write this book, and to Lea for reviewing early drafts and providing vital feedback. Your sharp mind and knowledge of what is currently needed in schools was instrumental in discerning how to shape this project.

Third, so many teens that I have taught over the last decade have shown me what works for them and what wasn't so critical to include in the curriculum. I have been both honored and humbled to share time with these teens and am so appreciative of their wisdom and contributions.

For those at PESI who helped to bring this idea into fruition: Kate Sample, Jenessa Jackson, and Linda Jackson. Kate, thank you for your guidance in getting this project started and through the editing process, and Jenessa, thank you for your careful eye, your patience, and your incredible ability to attend to every last detail. Linda, thank you for shepherding this through to the final product.

Finally, to my beloved partner, Dale. I can't imagine being able to accomplish anything—let alone writing a book—without your constant support and unlimited patience. I am grateful every day that you are in my life.

About the Author

Karen Bluth, PhD, is an associate professor in the Department of Psychiatry at the University of North Carolina at Chapel Hill. After leaving an 18-year career as a classroom teacher in elementary and middle schools to earn her PhD in child and family studies from the University of Tennessee in 2012, Dr. Bluth has spent the last decade researching how mindfulness and self-compassion can help teens navigate the challenging developmental period of adolescence. She co-created the program Mindful Self-Compassion for Teens, which teaches teens how they can be kinder and more supportive to themselves, and has found that teens are less depressed, anxious, and stressed after the program is over. The classroom version found in this book has been modified and expanded from the Mindful Self-Compassion for Teens program.

Dr. Bluth is one of the developers of the Mindful Self-Compassion for Educators program and Embracing Your Life: A Mindful Self-Compassion Program for Young Adults, and trains teachers in this program internationally. She is also the author of *The Self-Compassion Workbook for Teens: Mindfulness and Compassion Skills to Overcome Self-Criticism and Embrace Who You Are* and *The Self-Compassionate Teen: Mindfulness and Compassion Skills to Conquer Your Critical Inner Voice*, as well as co-author of *Mindfulness and Self-Compassion for Teen ADHD: Build Executive Functioning Skills, Increase Motivation, and Improve Self-Confidence* and the Audible Original *Self-Compassion for Girls: A Guide for Parents, Teachers, and Coaches*. In addition, she is the recipient of the inaugural Mind & Life Award for Public Communication of Contemplative Research, which was awarded in 2022.

A dedicated mindfulness practitioner for over 40 years, Dr. Bluth frequently gives talks, presents workshops, and teaches classes in the local community as well as internationally. She is the parent of two adult daughters and lives on the marsh on the coast of North Carolina with her b'sharta Dale, her beloved pup Izzy, and her 20-year-old cat Layla. She gets great joy from kayaking and observing the animal life on the marsh.